Ontario Dept. of Crown Lands

The Algoma District

and that part of the Nipissing District north of the Mattawan River, Lake

Nipissing and French River, their resources, agricultural and mining

capabilities. Prepared under instructions from the Commissioner of Crown

Lands

Ontario Dept. of Crown Lands

The Algoma District
*and that part of the Nipissing District north of the Mattawan River, Lake Nipissing
and French River, their resources, agricultural and mining capabilities. Prepared
under instructions from the Commissioner of Crown Lands*

ISBN/EAN: 9783337273002

Printed in Europe, USA, Canada, Australia, Japan

Cover: Foto ©Andreas Hilbeck / pixelio.de

More available books at **www.hansebooks.com**

THE

ALGOMA DISTRICT,

AND THAT PART OF THE

NIPISSING DISTRICT NORTH OF THE MATTAWA RIVER,
LAKE NIPISSING AND FRENCH RIVER, THEIR
RESOURCES, AGRICULTURAL AND
MINING CAPABILITIES.

> " Far as the heart can wish, the fancy roam,
> Survey our empire, and behold our home."

THE Algoma District is one of the most important divisions of the Province of Ontario.*

Its boundaries, as originally defined, were as follows :—" Commencing on the north shore of the Georgian Bay of Lake Huron at the most westerly mouth of French River, thence due north to the northerly limit of the Province, thence along the said northerly limit of the Province westerly to the westerly limit thereof, thence along the said westerly limit of the Province southerly to the southerly limit thereof, thence along the said southerly limit of the Province to a point in Lake Huron opposite to the southern extremity of the Great Manitoulin Island, thence easterly and north-easterly so as to include all the islands in Lake Huron not within the settled limits of any county or district, to the place of beginning."

By Proclamation of 13th May, 1871, the Territorial District of Thunder Bay was defined as " All that part of the District of Algoma lying west of the meridian of 87° of west longitude." This meridian is a little to the east of the Slate Islands in Lake Superior, and near the mouth of Steel River.

---

* Ontario—A poetic Indian name, signifying a beautiful prospect of hills and waters. The word " Algoma " means " Lake and Land of Algons," or Algonquin tribe of Indians.

NORTHERLY AND WESTERLY BOUNDARIES OF ONTARIO.
AWARD OF THE ARBITRATORS.

To all to whom these Presents shall come :

The undersigned having been appointed by the Governments of Canada and Ontario as arbitrators to determine the northerly and westerly boundaries of the Province of Ontario, do hereby determine and decide that the following are and shall be such boundaries ; that is to say :—

Commencing at a point on the southern shore of Hudson's Bay, commonly called James' Bay, where a line produced due north from the head of Lake Temiscaming would strike the said south shore; thence along the said south shore westerly to the mouth of the Albany River ; thence up the middle of the said Albany River, and of the lakes thereon, to the source of the said river at the head of Lake St. Joseph ; thence by the line to the easterly end of Lac Seul, being the head waters of the English River ; thence westerly through the middle of Lac Seul and the said English River to a point where the same will be intersected by a true meridional line drawn northerly from the international monument placed to mark the most north-westerly angle of the Lake of the Woods by the recent Boundary Commission ; and thence due south, following the said meridional line to the said international monument ; thence southerly and easterly following upon the international boundary line between the British possessions and the United States of America, into Lake Superior.

But if a true meridional line drawn northerly from the said international boundary at the said most north-westerly angle of the Lake of the Woods, shall be found to pass to the west of where the English River empties into the Winnipeg River, then, and in such case, the northerly boundary of Ontario shall continue down the middle of the said English River to where the same empties into the Winnipeg River, and shall continue thence on a line drawn due west from the confluence of the said English River with the said Winnipeg River, until the same will intersect the meridian above described ; and thence due south, following the said meridional line to the said international monument ; thence southerly and easterly, following upon the international boundary line, between the British possessions and the United States of America, into Lake Superior.

Given under our hands, at Ottawa, in the Province of Ontario, this third day of August, 1878.

Signed and published in the presence of   ROBT. A. HARRISON.

     E. C. MONK.   EDWD. THORNTON.

     THOMAS HODGINS.   F. HINCKS.

This vast territory is about 760 miles in length, with a breadth of 370 miles, and is situated principally between the 46th and 51st parallels of north latitude, and the 79th and 95th of longitude west from Greenwich. It contains about 200,000 square miles, or 130,000,000 of acres of land and water.

Its endless variety of hill and valley, river and lake, rapid, cascade and waterfall, is unrivalled in the world.

But not only is it great in respect to its area. Its soil furnishes unparalleled diversity of wealth. The miner is invited to the development of its mineral riches, hidden for ages; its plains and fertile valleys bid the husbandman welcome; and industries, in their manifold branches, stand waiting the command of intelligence and energy, without respect to nationality or social condition.

It is only of late years that attention has been directed to this new field for enterprise and development. In a very short time it will be traversed throughout its length from Lake Nipissing to Rat Portage, by the main line of the Canadian Pacific Railway, with a branch from Sudbury Junction to Algoma Mills on Lake Huron; and other lines are projected from Michipicoten and Lake Nipissing to James' Bay.

This region is drained by two grand water systems having their source in what is known as the Height of Land, which extends from Lake Abittibe on the east, to Lake St. Joseph on the west, and varies from 1,000 to 1,500 feet above the level of the sea. Those rivers running southward flow into the Great Lakes and the River St. Lawrence, and those running northward empty their waters into Hudson's Bay.

To intending settlers this country possesses many important advantages over the more distant prairies of the west—proximity to leading markets; the abundance and purity of its waters; the ample supply and cheapness of timber for building, fencing and fuel; and the greater cheapness of implements, clothing, etc.

SURFACE OF THE COUNTRY.

The whole of the territory south of the Height of Land is watered by numerous large and small rivers, and innumerable lakes and lakelets.

The characteristics of these rivers are much modified by the nature of the geological formations through which they pass, and the different powers of resistance of these formations to the transporting and eroding effect of the water.

In a formation composed of the harder crystalline rocks which obtrude themselves above the surface, the waters have not the same power to form for themselves channels as in a country based upon sedimentary deposits.

The irregular depressions and clefts in the surface of the Huronian formation become filled with water, and form lakes, whose overflow tumbles in cascades and rapids, and finds its way into other lakes lying at a lower level, until it is received into Lake Huron or Superior. In this district the country is dotted with lakes, and the connecting rivers are generally short. The navigation, in this northern river system, consists of stretches of deep and still water, interrupted by rapids and falls, around which the light canoes of the voyageurs are portaged by hand.

This river system, fortunately for us, is thus furnished with a series of reservoirs, which cannot be destroyed, in the lakes themselves. These lakes receive the waters from rain and the melting of the snows in the spring, and hold them stored up against the summer·heat.

Through the rocks of this region run numerous bands of crystalline limestone or marble, which from their softness give rise to valleys with a fertile soil. The hill-sides are generally covered with vegetable mould which sustains a growth of trees, giving them an aspect of luxuriant vegetation. But when fire has passed over these hills, the soil is in great part destroyed, and the rock is soon laid bare. In the valleys and lower parts, however, there are large areas of good land, having a deep soil and bearing heavy timber. These are the chief lumbering districts of the country, and constitute a great source of wealth to the Province. In these regions the occupations of the lumberer and the farmer are a great encouragement to one another, as the wants of the lumberman afford to the farmer a ready market for his produce at high prices.

There are many reasons why the forest-region of the hills should be protected by the settler. The vegetation and the soil which now cover the hillsides play a most important part in retaining the waters which here fall in the shape of rain or snow. But for this covering of the soil, the rivers and mill-streams which here take their rise, would, like the streams of Southern France, and of the North of Italy, be destructive torrents at certain seasons, and almost dried-up channels at others. The effect of this great wooded area in tempering the winds and moderating the extremes of climate, must not be overlooked by the settler in estimating the value of his homestead.

COUNTRY NORTH OF THE MATTAWA RIVER AND LAKE NIPISSING.

Geological Features—Sequence of the Formations.

That part of the Ottawa River which lies between its tributary the Mattawa, and a point about three miles south of the mouths of the Montreal and Metabechuan Rivers, appears to cross the axis of an anticlinal arch, which separates the rim of the great southern trough of fossiliferous formations of which the western geological area of Ontario has been described as forming but a part, from a northern trough, whose strata probably run under the waters of Hudson's Bay.

The lowest rocks which this undulation brings to the surface are of a highly crystalline quality, belonging to the order which, in the nomenclature of Lyell is called metamorphic instead of primary, as possessing an aspect inducing a theoretic belief that they may be ancient sedimentary formations in an altered condition. Their general character is that of a syenitic gneiss. Their general colour is reddish, and it arises from the presence of reddish feldspar, which is the prevailing constituent mineral. The feldspar, however, is often white, and frequently of a bluish grey. The rock is in no case without quartz. Hornblende is seldom absent, and mica very often present. The prevailing colour of the quartz is white, but it is often transparent or translucent. The hornblende is usually black and sometimes green. The mica is often black, frequently brown, and generally of a dark tinge. The rock (carefully distinguished from dykes), is almost universally small grained, and though the constituent minerals are arranged in parallel layers, no one constituent so monopolises any layer as to exclude the presence of others; but even in their subordinate arrangement there is an observable tendency to parallelism. A thick bed of reddish feldspathic rock, for example, will in section present a number of short dashes of black hornblende or black mica, all drawn in one direction, destitute of arrangement, apparently, except in regard to their parallelism; or it will be marked by parallel dotted lines composed of these minerals. The continuation of these lines will be interrupted irregularly, and before one ends another will commence above or below it, the lines interlocking among one another. Sometimes thin continuous parallel black belts will run in the rock for considerable distances; or, it will be barred by parallel streaks of white quartz or white feldspar, in which, as well as the red part, these dark and dotted lines will occur. The same description of arrangement will be found where the whole ground of the rock is white instead of red, and then the red feldspar will occasionally constitute streaks. There is no end to the diversity of arrangement in which the minerals and the colours will be observed.

While the subordinate contents of beds will be thus arranged, masses will be divided into beds shewing nearly as great a diversity. The beds will be sometimes very thick, and these usually are of the red variety of rock ; at others they will be thin, and the hornblende or the mica, or both, will be the dominant minerals, or equal the others in quantity. In this case the mass will present a light or dark grey colour, and the mica, rendering the rock fissile, will cause it to yield good flagging or tile stones. The reddish feldspathic masses are stronger and more solid than the others, yielding less to the influence of the weather, and when their bulk is considerable they rise into hills, and largely prevail in all the ranges met with. The thin bedded rocks often constitute the valleys.

The dip of the strata is usually at high angles, and towards the Mattawa it appears to point more generally southward. But there evidently exist many undulations, often accompanied by contortions. Some of the undulations give northern and sometimes eastern dips. It is not supposed, however, that these undulations have any dependent connection with the anticlinal axis, or, that its position will be peculiarly marked by any of them. The arch is of two gentle a nature to have produced any palpable change in the slope of the highly tilted strata, and it is probable that these had assumed their twists and undulations before the existence of the arch, and that the forces producing it operated on the wrinkled mass merely as a whole, without, in any very preceptible degree, affecting the relation of its parts.

Ascending Lake Temiscaming, the slates come in upon the gneiss about three miles below the mouths of the Montreal and Metabechuan rivers on the west bank, and about three miles above them on the east ; and they occupy both sides to within two and a-half miles of the Hudson Bay Company's post. In this distance they may have a direct breadth of about seven miles, in which they are affected by at least one undulation, and constitute hills of 300 to 400 feet. These slates run in a westerly direction forty miles, in a line about S. 40 W. from Lake Temiscaming to Bass Lake, on the Sturgeon River, which discharges into Lake Nipissing on the north side, and it is probable they come out on some part of the north shore of Lake Huron. On Lake Temiscaming they are followed by the sandstones, which cross the lake with a strike of N. 60° E., and dipping northward at a very small angle, after having been piled up into a range of about the same elevation as the slate hills, they reach the Company's Post, where, nearly flat, they run under a narrow gravel hill 130 feet in height: emerging beyond, they continue to a distance of about half a mile above the post, and are then interrupted on both sides of the lake by a mass of syenite. This syenite does not possess the gneissoid arrangement of the rock lower down the river, but it appears to be nearly similar in other respects, being composed of reddish feldspar, white or colourless quartz, and a sparing quantity of green hornblende. The breadth of this syenitic band is pretty nearly three miles on both sides of the lake. On the west it is succeeded by the sandstones, which run along the coast for a distance of four miles, nearly on the strike of the measures, dipping towards the water at a small angle, and are followed by the slates which come from behind them, and continue in a straight line for nine miles to the western bay at the head of the lake, forming high perpendicular cliffs for part of the way and rounded hills for the remainder.

The limestones constitute the two large islands near the head of the lake, the two smaller ones between them, the island at the entrance of the eastern bay and a very small one on the west coast, as well as the promontory which separates the east bay from the west. The strata lie in the form of a shallow trough, based sometimes on the sandstones and sometimes on the slates, occupying the breadth of the lake—from five to six miles—and extending from the south side of the southern great island to some unknown distance northward, being either a projecting point or an outlier of some more extended calcareous area.

The largest and best quality of flagging slabs is found on the east side of Lake Temiscaming, about seven miles above the Galere, where five miles of the coast present a succession of cliffs which would yield a great abundance of almost any dimensions. Roofing slates exist about five miles up the Montreal River.

Lakes, Rivers and Agricultural Capabilities.

On the north bank of the Mattawa a range of hills, of no great elevation, runs nearly the whole way from Trout Lake to the mouth, and between their base and the margin of the water there are good mixed wood flats, with elm, ash, maple, and a few oaks; but the slopes produce soft woods chiefly, the prevailing species being red pine.

To the north of Upper Trout Lake there is an extensive spread of flat hard-wood country running in an east and west direction, possessing a good soil, consisting of loam in some places and clay in others, and the timber, in a great measure, composed of black birch, maple, and basswood.

Associated with this tract is another, at the distance of five miles on the west side of Seven League Lake, on the Ottawa between the Mattawa River and Lake Temiscaming, running in a south-westerly course to the vicinity of the Mattawa, and reaching as high as the Galere on Lake Temiscaming, though it is not there much nearer the lake than it approaches the river lower down.

Lake Temiscaming, a magnificent stretch of navigable water, the largest and deepest on the whole course of the Ottawa, extends seventy-five miles without any obstruction to vessels of the largest tonnage. It consists of three lakes, the lower, middle and upper, connected by narrow straits.

The Upper Lake extends from Fort Temiscaming to the "Head." This beautiful sheet of water has all the characteristics of a true lake. It is from six to eight miles wide, indented with deep bays, bold promontories, steep cliffs and low banks, and is studded with picturesque islands, two of which are of considerable size.

The Montreal River, its largest tributary as regards both extent and volume, takes its source at the northern Height of Land, flows for about sixty miles in an easterly direction, and sixty miles more south-easterly, discharges into Middle Lake by several mouths.

The river Blanche, which derives its name from the white or turbid colour of its water, discharges into Lake Temiscaming at its "Head," and is navigable for twenty-five miles. The area of the clay land drained by this river has been estimated to be between 500 and 600 square miles, equivalent to twelve townships of fifty square miles, or 32,000 acres each. This is the largest area of land fit for settlement, in one unbroken clay block, in the unsettled portion of Ontario.

The limit southward of this tract of good level country is associated with a change occurring in the quality of the rock formations of the district in the vicinity of the mouth of the Montreal River on the right side of the lake, and a few miles higher up on the left. The unbroken monotony of the hard syenitic gneiss, constituting so much of the banks of the lake and main river further down, here ceases; a more distinctly stratified set of rocks, of a less crystalline and more easily disintegrating character, presents itself. The ranges of the hills become more determinate, the valleys wider, and many of them are occupied by clay lands. At its very extremity both sides of the lake present a favourable aspect; good stratified limestone there makes its appearance, constituting the large islands already mentioned, and the promontory separating the east and west bays. Its escarpment does not exceed 100 feet, and it runs northward into the interior with an even continuity of height, which can be followed by the eye for miles.

The marshes, arising from the sediment deposited by the Blanche and other rivers at their mouths, are extensive, and produce an abundant supply of good meadow hay.

The general character of the country south and east of Lake Tamagamingue is undulating but not very broken. This lake is a fine sheet of very clear water, abounding with bass, pickerel, pike, and salmon trout, and filled with islands. The scenery is beautiful, resembling that of the Thousand Islands of the St. Lawrence. This lake has two outlets, one flowing south into the Sturgeon River, which empties into Lake Nipissing, and the other flowing north into the Montreal River, which discharges into Lake Temiscaming. Numerous lakes, of various sizes, are dotted at intervals over this country. Otter Tail Creek is the principal stream falling into the Ottawa.

Throughout the whole of this region there is good clay soil along the flats of the rivers and creeks; generally, however, a sandy loam prevails.

After traversing the township of Widdifield, on the north-east shore of Lake Nipissing, the land descends gradually to the north, showing a level country of hard-wood timber, with here and there some rock, and generally a good loamy soil.

Turning east, between townships 17 and 13,* on the nineteenth mile from the boundary of Springer, the country is flat in some places, but generally undulating with fair soil. From the twenty-first to the forty-fourth mile on this line, there is a good tract of country with rolling land and good soil, fit for farming purposes, the timber being chiefly maple and black birch of large growth and good quality, with some good scattering pine.

The Township of Widdifield (No. 17) is nearly all good hard-wood land, and is by far the best township in this section of the country. Finer hardwood bush is rarely seen. There are a few bass-wood trees, iron-wood in some places, and a grove of beech on the east boundary a few miles north of Trout Lake.

---

* These numbers have reference to an exploration made by the Department of Crown Lands in 1882, and are applied to townships lying east of the Township of Springer and the Indian Reserve, which, with the exception of Widdifield, have been outlined, but not surveyed or named.

Townships 22, 23, 27 and 28 contain a large percentage of good land, with considerable pine.

Townships 1, 5, 9, 13 and 18 also contain a fair percentage of good land, with very little pine. The timber is chiefly balsam, spruce, birch, with occasional patches of hardwood.

The Jocko River runs eastward through a fine tract of country to the River Ottawa.

Sturgeon River, emptying into Lake Nipissing, is a fine deep stream, having an average breadth of six chains to the first fall, about six miles from its mouth.

The Veuve, or Widow River, empties into Lake Nipissing, about four miles west of Sturgeon River.

Lake Nipissing lies immediately above the 46th parallel of latitude, and across the 80th of longitude. In form it is very irregular, but has an extreme length, east and west, of about forty miles, and a maximum breadth, north and south, of about twenty miles. Its area in round numbers is about 300 square miles.

The northerly shores of the lake are low, generally of flat rock and sand, and the water shoal upon a sandy bottom. Its waters pass out into French River by three distinct outlets through myriads of islands.

The French River, though sometimes merging into one vast lake, is, throughout the greater part of its length, divided into two main channels. From its entrance on Georgian Bay to its outlet on Lake Nipissing the distance is about forty miles, and the navigation is obstructed by falls and rapids. The scenery of the Thousand Isles of the St. Lawrence is tame and uninteresting as compared with the endless variety of island and bay, granite cliff, and deep sombre defile, which mark the character of the beautiful, solitary French River.

HEIGHTS ABOVE THE SEA.

The height of the surface of Lake Temiscaming at its head above the waters of the St. Lawrence at Three Rivers, which is about the highest point affected by the action of the tides, is 612 feet. The level of the Mattawa, at its junction with the Ottawa, is 519 feet 5 inches.

The height of the surface of Upper Trout Lake, the source of the Mattawa, is 690 feet, and of the Height of Land between it and the Vase River on the canoe portage, is 714 feet 5 inches.

The fall from the height of land to the River Vase at the end of the portage is 22 feet 11 inches, and from this point to Lake Nipissing, the fall is 26 feet 6 inches, which makes the height of Lake Nipissing above the waters of the St. Lawrence at Three Rivers, 665 feet.

The ascertained height of the surface of Lake Huron above the sea, according to the Michigan surveyors, is 578 feet.

NORTH SHORE OF LAKE HURON.

General View.

The north shore of Lake Huron presents an undulating country, rising into hills which sometimes attain the height of 400 and 700 feet above the lake. These occasionally exhibit rugged escarpments, and naked rocky surfaces; but in general their summits are rather rounded, and their flanks, with the valleys separating one range from another, are most frequently well clothed with hard and soft wood, often of large growth, and of such species as are valuable in commerce; in many places giving promise of a good arable soil.

To the westward of Spanish River the coast is for the most part low; it abounds with safe and commodious harbours among its numerous islands and inlets, which can scarcely fail in many instances to become, in course of time, of commercial importance. To the eastward of the river the scenery is improved by the gradual approach of a high range of picturesque hills coming out upon the coast. They are known as the La Cloche mountains, one of their highest points being 482 feet above the level of the lake. This part of the lake is thickly studded with islands, and the coast is much indented with extensive bays and inlets which offer shelter and security during any storm to which the voyager may be exposed.

The general features of the country bordering on the River St. Mary and Lake Huron, are very similar; at times, bold, rugged, and declivitous, and scantily clothed with stunted spruce, balsam, pine, and birch, the coast affords but little land fit for agricultural purposes; at others, rising gently from the margin of the water, and covered with a fair growth of hardwood timber, birch, maple, and iron-wood, it holds out inducements to the explorer to penetrate before condemning; whilst here and there, extensive tracts of level land are seen, in some places low and swampy, presenting an almost impenetrable thicket of black alder and sallow; in others, open prairie, covered with a luxuriant growth of wild grass.

Leaving the shores of the river or lake, at distances varying from two to five miles, the scene changes; and the topographical features of the country may be described as consisting of rich alluvial valleys, varying in width from a quarter to seven miles, heavily timbered with mixed timber; crossed at intervals by rock ridges, and traversed by small rivulets of excellent water. These ridges, with the exception of Gros Cap and La Cloche, form no regular mountain range, but are short escarpments of rock, seldom more than three-fourths of a mile in length, and varying in height from 30 to 250 feet, rounded on the flanks, and although bold and declivitous on the southerly side, are, on the north, easy of approach, as the descent from the summit is regular, and the side generally well timbered with hardwood.

In the valleys the soil is, generally, decayed vegetable matter, or a rich sandy loam, with a subsoil of reddish blue or white clay; in many instances resembling limestone in a state of decomposition; the timber mixed and consisting of birch, maple, iron-wood, cedar, elm, ash, pine, spruce, balsam, hemlock, and poplar, according to the locality.

Geological Features.

The series of rocks occupying this country from the connecting link between Lakes Huron and Superior to the vicinity of Shebanahning* a distance of 120 miles, with a breadth in some places of ten, and in others exceeding 20 miles, must be taken as belonging to one formation. On the west it seems to repose on the granite, running to the east of Gros Cap north of Sault Ste. Marie; on the east the same supporting granite is observed north of La Cloche, between three and four miles in a straight line up the Riviere au Sable, a south flowing tributary of the Spanish River; and again, about an equal distance up another and parallel tributary joining that stream eight miles further from its mouth, in both cases about ten miles from the coast. The series is to be divided into rocks of a sedimentary, and rocks of an igneous origin.

The sedimentary portion consists of sandstones, conglomerates, slates and limestones. The sandstones are sometimes grey, but more generally white, almost purely silicious and principally fine grained, but the granular texture is often lost, and great masses assuming a vitreous lustre present the character of a perfect quartz rock which is met with of both the colours mentioned, and when white it sometimes exhibits precisely the aspect of the milky or greasy quartz of mineralogists. The quartz rock, in addition to white and grey, is not unfrequently of a reddish color, and sometimes a

---

* Killarney.

decided red. In the granular varieties considerable masses of the rock sometimes present a white with a faint tinge of sea-green, which seems to arise from a small quantity of finely disseminated epidote. The rock often becomes coarse grained, assuming the character of a conglomerate, the pebbles of which vary from the size of duck-shot to that of grape and canister. These pebbles are almost entirely either of opaque white vitreous quartz or various coloured jaspers; some few are of lydian stone, and some of hornstone and other varieties. The pebbles are often disposed in their layers at the top or bottom, or in the midst of finer grained beds; but they are sometimes arranged in thicker bands, which swell into mountain masses, *and blood-red jaspers often disseminated in these to a preponderating degree on a nearly pure white ground, giving a brilliant, unique and beautiful rock, appear to characterize some ranges of considerable importance.*

The igneous rocks may be classed, as a whole, under the denomination of greenstone trap. The masses they present are sometimes very great, and in such cases the trap usually consists of a greenish-white feldspar, and dark-green or black hornblende.

The limestone has not been seen in contact with any of the greenstone overflows; but on Echo Lake there is a great body of greenstone over it to the south, with a thick band of syenitic conglomerate associated with quartz rock interposed between them and a range of quartz hills above. On the Thessalon Lakes, great mountain masses of quartz rock, with subordinate jasper conglomerates, appear to underlie the limestone, and at La Cloche a band of 3,000 to 4,000 feet rests upon it.

Metalliferous veins intersect all the rocks that have been mentioned. Slips, or displacements, of the country on opposite sides of the veins occur when fissures are found that constitute their mould or receptacle. Numerous instances are observed where both granite and greenstone dykes, cut by the metalliferous veins, are suddenly heaved considerably out of their course. This fact may be deemed valuable as shewing the probable great depth and distance to which the veins may run.

The metal which these veins hold in the greatest quantity is copper, and the ores in which it occurs are vitreous copper, variegated copper, and copper pyrites. Iron pyrites is sometimes associated with them, but, in general, not in large quantity. Copper pyrites is, in some instances, accompanied by rutile, and in others by the arsenuretted sulphuret of iron and nickel, containing a trace of cobalt. The gangue, or vein stone, in which the copper ores are contained, is, in general, white quartz, and there is very often present, but not in very great quantity, white compact dolomite, which in druses assumes the forms of pearl spar, and brown or bitter spar ; calc spar also appears occasionally in druses in dog-tooth crystals.

The veins vary in breadth from a few inches to sometimes thirty feet, but when of this last great breadth, or even much less, they usually contain a considerable amount of brecciated wall-rock mixed up with the gangue ; many of them range from one to three and four feet, and their slope, or underlie varies, from about 50° to 90°. From such as might be considered master lodes innumerable branches of various sizes start, some of which visibly diminish before proceeding far, and dwindle to nothing, while others maintain moderate widths with much regularity for considerable distances, and may run to a junction with parallel lodes. The lodes have a bearing agreeing with the general strike of the formation, which roughly coincides with the general trend of the coast. They are thus, in a rude way, parallel to one another, and run in a direction between west and north-west, more nearly approaching the latter.

In no part of the country, from the vicinity of Sault Ste Marie to Shebanahning, is any great area wholly destitute of cupriferous veins, and it would appear singular if a region, extending over a space of between one and two thousand square miles, and so marked by indications, did not in the course of time yield many valuable results.

Rivers, Agricultural Capabilities, Timber, &c.

Six principal rivers, besides several of inferior note, flow through this country, The principal are the Thessalon, the Mississaga, the Serpent, the Spanish, the White Fish, and the Wahnapitael, of which the mouths are from fifteen to thirty miles apart. The Mississaga and the Spanish are the largest two, the reported length of the former being 120 and of the latter 200 miles.

In the valleys of all the principal streams there are extensive flats of rich and deep soil, producing maple, oak, elm, birch and basswood, besides occasional groves of both red and white pine of large size.

From Sault Ste. Marie to Root River, the surface is generally level, with a slight inclination to the eastward, or towards Garden River ; the soil is here a fine sandy loam, and the subsoil a reddish blue clay.

Root River, flowing south-easterly, is a small stream, emptying into the St. Mary River on the westerly side of Little Lake George ; it is shallow, with clear water, rapid current, and gravel bottom. The soil on both sides of the river is good. Northward of the river for six miles, the surface is gently undulating, broken here and there by the rock ridges previously described, the soil and timber being the same as on the south side.

In rear of this, a valley of seven or eight miles in width extends eastward to the high land surrounding Echo Lake, and westward to the Gros Cap Range at the foot of Lake Superior, its regularity broken here and there by similar ranges of rock.

Garden River, flowing southerly and south-westerly, empties into the St. Mary River a short distance eastward of Little Lake George. It is a fine stream, having a general width of about three chains. Here, wheat, oats, maize, potatoes, and grass, grow luxuriantly. The soil on the banks of this river, and for a considerable distance inland on either side is of the best quality, being a fine rich sandy loam, and the timber is large and thrifty.

The valley, entered northward from Root River, is again seen presenting the same appearance, and stretching eastward to the high land surrounding Echo Lake. Through each of these valleys there usually flows a pretty brook of clear water, taking its rise from one or other of the picturesque little lakes which lie on each side of the water shed.

To the east of Echo Lake, and northward of the limestone point on the east side, there is a tract of fine land, heavily timbered with maple, elm and birch, interspersed at intervals with groves of hemlock and a few pines, with cedars in the hollows and swamps.

The Thessalon River, with its chain of lakes and mill-sites, flowing from the north-west, empties into Lake Huron about twelve miles eastward of the Bruce Mines.

The land on the margin of the river is of good quality and heavily timbered. The surface rises gently from the water's edge, and at the top of the bank the rock is exposed; this continues, however, but a short distance, when it descends gradually, and for several miles to the eastward the soil is of good quality and deep, the surface rolling, and the timber fine and thrifty, maple, birch, cedar, elm and ash prevailing. Much good pine is also scattered through this section.

Westward of the river, or in rear of the Bruce Mines, the country is more broken and rugged. North and west from Desert Lake, the second of the chain, the coast is low and swampy for the distance of three-quarters of a mile, but in rear the surface rises gradually, and, though broken here and there by the rock ranges which form a marked feature in the topography of this country, affords a considerable extent of land fit for settlement, the soil being deep and rich, and the timber principally hardwood.

North and east from Lake Deception, the third of the series, there are extensive tracts of excellent land, timbered chiefly with hardwood ; these tracts extend eastward to the Mississaga, and southward to within two miles of the coast of Lake Huron.

The Mississaga River, entering Lake Huron about thirty miles eastward of Point Thessalon is, at its entrance into the lake, a fine broad stream, with a considerable depth of water, and its mouth being protected eastward by several islands affords a safe and commodious harbour. The navigation is, however, impeded four miles from its mouth, where a rock range, crossing the river, forms a fall of five feet.

At the mouth of the river the land is low and swampy, but the surface rises gradually, and at the distance of one and a half miles from the lake the banks on both sides are high, and the soil and timber of good quality, the former being a rich red sand with a subsoil of blue clay, and the latter consisting of birch, hard and soft maple, cedar, poplar, spruce, balsam, black and white ash, and elm.

Between the northerly limit of the Indian Reserve and Little White River, a south-west flowing tributary of the Mississaga, there is a tract of country of considerable extent fit for settlement. Northward of Little White River there is a fine block of land extending nearly to the Grand Portage, and stretching to the eastward for a considerable distance.

The Blind River, forming the eastern limit of the Indian Reserve, enters Lake Huron about four miles east of the Mississaga.

Serpent River empties into a deep bay or inlet of Lake Huron about twenty-five miles east of the Mississaga. The bay into which it empties is unsurpassed as a harbour. At the mouth of the river, on the westerly side, the land is of good quality, but low and level. Ascending the river the scene is rugged and rough, the rock ranges running close to the margin of the stream and parallel to it. In rear, however, on both sides some valleys of good hardwood land are met with, more particularly on the west, being a continuation of the valleys from the east bank of the Mississaga.

Spanish River, which is navigable for thirty miles to craft not drawing over five feet, falls into an extensive and beautiful bay, land-locked by islands and projecting points from the main land, the communication to the eastward being through a narrow but deep channel, called the Petit Detroit, between the southern extremity of the peninsula and the eastern end of Aird Island. From the Petit Detroit to La Cloche the outline of the coast is irregular, being indented by deep bays and coves, which in some parts are perfectly landlocked by groups of long, low and narrow islands running parallel with the main shore, and affording excellent places of shelter for all classes of vessels under almost any circumstances.

The hills bordering on Spanish River seldom attain a height over 300 feet, but the banks of the river itself are frequently bold, precipitous and rocky. At the great fall a picturesque and imposing ruggedness prevails. A ridge of smoothly polished bare rock rises in rounded knolls, so steep in places, as to be inaccessible, obstructing the south-eastern flow of the river and splitting it into two parts, of which one turns a little to the northward of east, while the other is deflected to a precisely opposite course. The latter, after running above a quarter of a mile, is thrown in a beautiful cascade over a precipice thirty feet high, and then turning abruptly to the eastward rushes violently for thirty chains in that direction, falling in a vertical sheet over three successive steps of five feet each, when it is again united to the other division of the stream in a wide pool of nearly still water.

Much of the country for some distance back from the north side of the river is flat or rolling land, and is almost everywhere covered with a luxuriant growth of red and white pine.

The extent and value of the pine forest in this region, the facility offered by the river for navigation, the water-power to be found on the main stream and all its tributaries, and the capabilities of the soil for raising most of the necessaries of life, all tend to indicate a probability that it is destined to become of commercial importance to the Province.

The White-fish River in its whole length, until within a mile or less of Lake Huron, consists of a long chain of lakes lying at short distances from one another, connected by short, small and sometimes rapid streams.

The valley of the Wahnapitæ River contains many considerable tracts of flat land, much of which is of good quality, bearing hardwood and large white pine in abundance, but a great proportion of the flats are low, wet and swampy.

The Vermilion River is a fine broad stream with deep water and a rapid current, which, flowing generally south-westerly, empties into Vermilion Lake, and thence running southerly, joins the east branch of the Spanish River about five miles east of White-fish Lake. The banks of the Vermillion River present a very inviting appearance both as regards soil and timber, the former being a rich alluvial deposit with a subsoil of reddish blue clay, and the latter principally fine and thrifty hardwood. Inland for a considerable distance from its banks the same appearance prevails, white oak, elm, and white ash being abundant.

2

This river takes its rise near the Height of Land, and unlike most of the streams in this country, is unbroken save by the one lake above spoken of.

Vermilion Lake is a long, narrow sheet of water timbered to the water's edge with birch, poplar, maple and oak, and takes its name from the peculiarly beautiful colour of the foliage in the autumn.

Grain, root crops and Indian corn flourish here to perfection.

On the south side of the Height of Land, and coming down in some places to within a few miles of Lake Huron, the country, as before remarked, like that for a considerable distance north, is full of lakes. These are not generally very deep, one result of which is that the water heated by the sun's rays becomes much warmer throughout than the water of Lakes Huron and Superior. The climate of a wide belt of territory is so tempered and modified by the warm waters of the numerous small and shallow lakes, which cover probably one-third of the country, as to admit of the cultivation of many of the most valuable kinds of fruit.

East of the Bruce Mines, in the valleys of the Thessalon and Mississaga Rivers, all kinds of crops flourish well. Spring wheat grows from four to five feet high and thick on the ground, yielding from twenty-five to thirty bushels to the acre. The oat crop is remarkably good, and yields from fifty to seventy bushels per acre. In this section of the country there is a good opening for stock raising, and stock farms with large clearances can be had at reasonable rates.

LAKE HURON AND THE MANITOULIN ISLANDS.

A ridge of land which, proceeding from the vicinity of the Falls of Niagara, sweeps round the upper extremity of Lake Ontario and running thence into the promontory of Cape Hurd and Cabot's Head, is represented in continuation by the Manitoulin Islands, divides Lake Huron into two parts, which may be called the south and the north. The south part, constituting the great body of the lake with a circumference exceeding 720 lineal miles, has an area of about 14,000 square miles; the north portion is again divided into two parts, the east and the west, the former of which, called the Georgian Bay, extending from Nottawasaga to Shebanahning and the eastern extremity of the Grand Manitoulin Island, with a length of 120 miles and a breadth of 50, has an area of about 6,000 square miles; while the remainder, called the north channel, gradually narrowing as it proceeds westward, presents a surface, exclusive of the various islands with which it is studded, particularly in the eastern end, of 1,700 square miles. The whole area of the water of the lake would thus appear to be 21,000 square miles.

Only four of the islands which serve to divide the lake go under the denomination of the Manitoulins. These are Drummond (belonging to the United States), Cockburn, Grand Manitoulin, and Fitzwilliam. They belong geologically to the fossiliferous series, exhibiting the Trenton limestone, Niagara limestone, and Utica slates. The Manitoulin Islands were covered with dense forests of the description usually indicating a rich and fertile soil. On them, and on St. Joseph Island further west, there are extensive tracts of land almost exclusively growing maple, elm, oak, ash, birch and basswood, of such character in point of size as not to be greatly surpassed by the produce of the justly celebrated hard timber lands of Ontario. St. Joseph Island abounds in limestone, affording good material for either burning or building.

The Grand Manitoulin is a very important and very beautiful island. Its length is 80 and its average breadth 20 miles. The forty-sixth parallel of north latitude passes three of its most northern points, and the eighty-second and eighty-third meridians of west longitude are at about equal distances from its east and west ends. The whole area of the island, exclusive of its numerous bays and inlets, cannot be less than 1,600 square miles. Its most elevated points do not exceed 350 feet over the level of Lake Huron. The amount of moisture which falls in this area must be considerable, as the interior of the island is well supplied with streams and lakes.

LAKE SUPERIOR REGION.

General View.

The Canadian shores of Lake Superior in general present a bold and rocky coast, diversified in the character of its scenery in accordance with the distribution of its different geological formations. Cliffs and eminences rise up to heights varying from 300 to 1,350 feet (Thunder Cape) close upon its margin, and this, deeply indented in some parts with extensive bays, and in others presenting extensive clusters of islands, is, in a multitude of places, carved out into well sheltered coves and inlets, affording inumerable harbours of a safe and commodious character, destined greatly to facilitate the commerce of the lake, in the produce of its fields, mines and fisheries. The timber of the district, west of Cape Gargantua, does not promise much encouragement to traffic, as it is not of the size nor of the kinds most esteemed in commerce, though there is much useful wood for saw-milling purposes, capable of being rendered available for mining, house building, railway ties and fuel. Hardwood is scarce, red pine is not often seen, and white pine not abundant. The trees most common are spruce, balsam fir, white birch, and poplar, with cedar in moist places. On the immediate coast many of the hills are nearly denuded of trees, particularly where granite and gneiss prevail. The hills composed of trap are better clothed ; but it is in the trappean valleys and on the surfaces underlaid by sandstone, which are usually flat, that the largest growth is met with. It is in these localities also, and at the mouths of the principal rivers, that good land fit for cultivation is found, sufficient for the wants of a large population.

Several considerable streams fall into the lake, the chief of which are, the Kamanistiquia, the Neepigon, the Pic, the Michipicoten, the Agawa, the Montreal, the Batchawaung, and the Goulais. The first three flow in on the north, and the others on the east side, and the whole, taking their origin in the Height of Land, separating the waters of Hudson's Bay from those of the St. Lawrence, pass through 100 to 200 miles of country before yielding their tribute to the grand head reservoir of the latter, which, with a rim of 500 leagues, comprises an area of 32,000 square miles, its greatest length being 350 miles, and its greatest breadth 160 miles. Its greatest depth is supposed to be 1,200 feet, which would make its bottom 603 feet below, while its surface is 597 feet above the level of the sea ; and its mean depth being taken at 600 feet, would give about 4,000 cubic miles of water.

The frosts of winter are not sufficiently long to cool, nor the heats of summer to warm this great body of water to the temperature of the surrounding surface, and the lake in consequence considerably modifies the temperature of the country on its banks, which is neither so low in the one season nor so high in the other, as it is both to the east and to the west. In the middle of the lake, in the month of July, the temperature of the water at the surface is not much more than 39° fah., and the temperature of the atmosphere above the lake is no more than 51°, while in the interior of the country it is between 70° and 80° or more. The result of such differences is the great prevalence of fogs on the lake.

On the margin of the lake in several parts, and on the banks of some of the streams, considerable accumulations of drifted materials are observed consisting of clay, sand, gravel and boulders, derived from the ruin of rocks The organic remains met with in these belong to some of the pebbles composing the gravel, and these fossiliferous pebbles appear to have been derived from rocks not lower than the Niagara limestones. Some of these accumulations of drift reach the height of 330 feet above the level of the lake.

Geological Features.

Lake Superior appears to be situated in a geological depression, which presents formations of a similar character on both the north and south sides, dipping to the centre. The series on the north, in ascending order, consists of the following :—

1. Granite and syenite.
2. Gneiss.
3. Chloritic and partially talcose and conglomerate slates.
4. Bluish slates or shales, interstratified with trap.
5. Sandstones, limestones, indurated marls, and conglomerates, interstratified with trap.

Both the gneiss and the granite are very often traversed by an ancient system of dykes or veins of a granitic character, but there do not appear to be any metalliferous minerals associated with these veins.

Nearly all the formations mentioned are traversed by a vast collection of trap dykes which appear to be more durable than the rocks they cut, from which results a peculiarity in the geographical features of the country. The destructive action of the water upon the coast is partially arrested in its progress upon meeting with them, and the dykes which run with the strike are in consequence often found to shield the shore for considerable distances ; and it frequently happens that a narrow breach having been effected in a dyke, it will be found to be the entrance to a spacious cove worn out on each side in the softer rock behind it. In almost all these instances, commodious harbours are the result, and it is mainly owing to the presence of these dykes that so many such harbours exist on the Canadian side of the lake.

In addition to the dykes a vast collection of mineral veins intersect the formations of Lake Superior. A very large number of these contain a greater or smaller amount of various metalliferous ores, and the indications which they present are such as to render it probable that the country characterized by them will rise into importance as a mining region. The metals whose ores are met with are copper, lead, zinc and silver.

For the distance of about fifty miles west of the Michipicoten River, the slate and the granite rocks divide the coast. With the exception of a few square miles of the upper trap at Cape Gargantua, granite and gneiss appear to hold the coast all the way to the vicinity of Pointe aux Mines, a distance not far short of fifty miles, at the extremity of which they separate from the shore, maintaining a nearly straight south-easterly line across to the eastern part of Batchawaung Bay, leaving the trap of Mamainse between them and the lake. Thence they reach the northern part of Goulais Bay, and finally attain the promontory of Gros Cap, where they constitute a moderately bold range of hills, running eastwardly towards Lake Huron.

Michipicoten Island is a mass of amygdaloidal trap and sandstone belonging to the upper formation.

On the east side of the lake, white and read sandstones are seen at several points, and so also are beds of amygdaloidal trap with coarse inter-stratified conglomerates.

The age of the volcanic formations of Lake Superior has not been finally settled. The difficulty arises from the absence of fossils, none of a satisfactory kind having been obtained from any beds whose relation to the volcanic rocks is undoubted. The doubt concerning them seems to be whether they are older or newer than the Potsdam sandstone of New York. On St. Joseph Island, formations corresponding with the Utica slates and Trenton limestones with their characteristic fossils, are found resting upon other formations occupying the position and answering the conditions of the Calciferous and Potsdam sandstones, and there does not appear any reason to doubt that the last-mentioned rock reaches up to Sault Ste. Marie, and extends to the foot of the Gros Cap Mountain and Point Iroquois. The view taken of the sequence of these formations is, that the copper-bearing traps of Lake Superior are of a higher antiquity than the Potsdam sandstone.

The metalliferous lodes which characterize the rocks of this country are so numerous, and spread over so wide an area as to excite strong hopes of many valuable discoveries. In general, however, it is a mere narrow strip along the water line which has been examined. There is a reasonable foundation to expect that a period will arrive, which may be hastened by the construction of the Canadian Pacific Railway, when mining will become established as a permanent branch of industry in the region, and the extraction and reduction of its metalliferous ores will form a source of wealth to its future inhabitants.

Rivers, Soil, Timber, Agricultural Capabilities.

Between Salter's Lake Huron base line and the Goulais River, a distance of ten miles, there is a large proportion of good rolling land, occasionally broken by hills of trap rock, heavily timbered with maple, birch, balsam, spruce and some pine. The soil is a sandy loam, changing to rich clay loam in the valleys.

The Goulais River flows in a south-westerly direction through a valley varying from one and a-half to three miles in width, and empties itself into the bay of the same name. It is navigable for small boats for about twenty miles. For the first twelve or fifteen miles from its mouth the banks vary from five to twelve feet in height, and are in general of clay or gravel. The soil in the valley of the river is of excellent quality, giving growth to large maple, birch, elm, ash, and soft wood trees.

Leaving the Goulais River and proceeding north, the country for some miles resembles that just described. Hills are seen in some places from 300 to 600 feet in height, with green stone, trap and gneiss appearing on their summits in ragged cliffs ; while their flanks and the intervening valleys shew good loamy well timbered soil.

On approaching Lake Superior, the country, generally, is mountainous and barren.

Between Point Corbeau, on the north shore of Batchawaung Bay and Mamainse, there is a fine tract of richly-wooded land of some miles in width, and of a rich productive loam, giving growth to large maple, birch, oak, etc.

Batchawaung Bay affords a constant supply of the finest trout and white fish.

The surface of the country between Batchawaung Bay and Montreal River, though a good deal broken, contains in some places low hills, and valleys of good soil. The timber consists of spruce, balsam, maple, and birch, with some pine and tamarac. Iron is largely distributed over this district.

The Montreal, a clear rapid river, flows through several small lakes, and between high hills of granite and trap rocks, in a direction a little south of west. In the first ten miles from its mouth there is a succession of wild rapids and falls, varying from 10 to 150 feet in height, flowing through narrow gorges and openings in the rock.

The tract between the Montreal and Agawa Rivers is for the most part hilly, though valleys of good soil are sometimes met with. Maple begins to grow scarce in this latitude, the prevailing timber being spruce, birch and balsam.

The Agawa, a clear gravelly river, abounding in speckled trout, flows between high perpendicular cliffs of granite and greenstone in a direction a little west of south into Lake Superior, about six miles to the north of Montreal River The smaller streams of the country through which it flows, pour their contents in many cases, directly over cliffs 150 feet in height into this river.

From the Agawa to the Michipicoten River there is little change in the appearance of the country, or in the quality of the soil. Here, as well as in every other part of the Lake Superior District, the country is well watered by streams and lakes which contain many varieties of excellent fish.

The second river in point of size, on the north shore of Lake Superior, is the Michipicton. It is a large, clear, rapid river, and takes it rise far in the interior. It has been for many years the route taken by the Hudson's Bay Company's canoes in travelling to and from Hudson's Bay, and the principal trading establishment of the Company is at its mouth.

The Hudson's Bay Company's winter mail route to Sault Ste Marie connects in a nearly direct line the mouths of the Michipicoten and Agawa Rivers, and passes through 'a fine rolling country, well timbered with maple, birch, balsam and spruce, and watered by numerous streams and lakes.

The Pic River flows in a southerly direction for many miles, with a gentle current through a valley from one to three miles in width. The banks which are generally of clay, and low, rise in some places to 70 or 80 feet. There are many points on this river of rich clay soil, giving growth to elm, birch, poplar, and black ash of large size. All along the river blue clay, of the finest description, well adapted for the manufacture of bricks or fine pottery, may be got in abundance.

The Neepigon River, the largest on the north shore of Lake Superior, takes its rise in Lake Neepigon, flows through several smaller lakes, and empties itself through a wide deep channel into Neepigon Bay. At the eastern side of its entrance, bold precipitous greenstone cliffs, several hundred feet in height, overlie a red soft rock of a soapy structure, which is used in the manufacture of pipes. In the valleys between these cliffs and on the west side of the river, there is excellent soil heavily timbered. The water of this river is beautifully clear, and swarms with speckled trout, weighing from one to twelve pounds. About 30 miles up, Lake Neepigon is reached. This lake is 120 miles in length and 60 in breadth. Its surface is dotted with numerous islands, its waters are deep, and contain in abundance fish of every variety taken in Lake Superior.

In the Neepigon country the largest tract of good land appears to be on the south-western side of the lake. From the Nonwaten River, northward to the Pagitchigama, a distance of fifty miles, the country is comparatively level, and the soil generally fertile. This tract is represented as continuing nearly to the River Winnipeg, and becoming more generally level in receding from Lake Neepigon. The rivers entering in this part of Lake Neepigon, as far as examined, were found to flow with tortuous courses between muddy banks of clay, overspread with fine sand.

There is a considerable area of good land around the bottom of South and McIntyre's Bays, and on the peninsulas east of the latter Bay, and Gull Bay. From the mouth to the first rapid on the Poshkokagan, the loamy banks of the river are from twenty to thirty feet high. The River Kabitotiquia is so crooked that by following its windings from the mouth to the portage leading to Chief's Bays, the distance is estimated to be fully thirty miles, although it is only nine miles in a straight course. On both sides the country is level, and the soil sandy, supporting a growth of grass and bushes, the timber having been burnt off by repeated fires. The land is free from stones, and very little labour would be necessary to make it ready for the plough.

The Kaministiquia, the only river on the Canadian side of Lake Superior navigable for large vessels for any distance from its mouth, flows into Thunder Bay at Fort William. For the last fifteen miles of its course, it winds through a rich valley of alluvial soil, in the centre of the Townships of Neebing and Paipoonge, between banks varying from 5 to 40 feet in height, crowned with large elm, ash, poplar, birch, spruce and pine, with a thick underbrush of flowering shrubs.

Between its mouth and the Kakabeka Falls, which are scarcely inferior in grandeur to the Falls of Niagara, there is nothing in the flora to lead one to doubt the feasibility of raising all the cereals.

An exploratory survey, north of Lake Superior, made in 1870, shows a large tract of country fit for settlement, lying between the Michipicoten and Shequamka Rivers on the east and Pic River on the west.

In this region, the country near Lake Superior is generally rough and broken, with ranges of rocky hills, except in the valleys of the Michipicoten and Magpie Rivers, and between Michipicoten River and Lake Wawangonk, where the land is level, and of good alluvial sandy loam, in some places prairie land, cleared by fire. There is good level land also in the valley of the Shequamka River and Lake.

Between Lake Superior and Lake Matagoming, and the upper valley of the Magpie River, the land is generally undulating and rocky, but beyond that, it is comparatively level, with a soil of alluvial clay and sandy loam. The timber is generally white spruce, red pine, birch, poplar and cedar.

In the upper Magpie and Lake Esnogaming district there is good level land, of a rich alluvial clay loam, well wooded.

From Lake Esnogaming, westerly to White Lake, the land is generally level, with a soil of sandy loam, and in some places undulating and rocky.

In the White River valley there is excellent farming land, the soil being a rich alluvial deposit, well wooded with white spruce, red pine and large cedars. White Lake, through which White River flows, lies in a level region, well wooded, the soil being an alluvial sandy loam. This lake is 515 feet above the level of Lake Superior.

In the valley of the Black River, which flows into Pic River near Lake Superior, and connects with White Lake, the land is generally level, consisting of an alluvial loam, generally a rich clay loam, well wooded with large white spruce, poplar and cedar, with occasional exposures of gneiss, micaceous slate, etc.

North of the Black River, the soil is clay loam, level and well wooded. About eight miles above the Black River, a tract of most excellent farming land begins; the soil is a rich alluvial clay loam, supporting a luxuriant growth of timber, as well as, in many places, a fine growth of long prairie grass.

This fine tract of country with its fertile soil, continues upwards of fifty miles into the interior, where a wide extent of country, that has been burned off, with the same good land, stretches easterly and towards White Lake for a distance of about thirty miles.

The numerous lakes and rivers in the interior abound in excellent fish of many kinds.

The climate of this region is very favourable. From observations made at the Pic River, by Mr. Ironside of the Hudson's Bay Company, with a standard thermometer, the mean temperature was found to be—in July,

62° 88'; August, 63° 54'; September, 64° 19'; and October, 56° 02', with very fine weather during these months. Thus, although nearly five degrees of latitude north of Toronto, the temperature was nearly the same as at Toronto during July and August, and a few degrees warmer during September and October, taking the average of 29 years.

In a general way it may be said that the whole country which has been examined, north of the hilly region around Lake Superior, between the Pic River and Lake Neepigon, is comparatively level, with a sandy soil, generally dry, but in places interrupted by shallow swamps and low rocky ridges. The sand is underlaid by a light coloured clay which occasionally comes to the surface.

The drift, which has come from the north eastward, is rich in pebbles and boulders of the paleozoic limestones, which occur *in situ* in that direction. These are washed out and exposed in the banks of lakes, and along rivers and brooks, especially at rapids, and will prove valuable for burning into lime. The fossils which they contain are mostly silicified and indicate the Niagara formation.

In going from Lake Superior, through this country, to the valley of the Albany River, no difference is observed in the character of the vegetation, which may be accounted for by the greater elevation of the southern part, together with the cooling influence which Lake Superior exerts upon it. Oats and barley are successfully cultivated at Long Lake House ; while hay, potatoes, and all the ordinary vegetables thrive remarkably well. The potato-tops, as a rule, are not touched by frost up to the time of harvesting, which is during the first week in October.

RAINY RIVER, AND RAINY LAKE, LAKE OF THE WOODS, AND RAT PORTAGE.

This most important section of the Province lies between the Height of Land west of Lake Superior and the Winnipeg River.   In its general aspect it is a hilly and broken country, intersected by rapid rivers and wide-spread lakes.   The hills, however, do not rise to any great elevation, and there are several fine alluvial valleys, the most extensive of which is that of Rainy River.

The lakes and rivers present long reaches of navigable water, the principal of which, extending from Fort Frances to the western extremity of

Lac Plat, is 158 miles in length. Dense forests cover the whole of this region, and the most valuable kinds of wood are seen in various places and in considerable quantities. Elm is found on Rainy River, and white pine is abundant on the waters which flow towards Rainy Lake. On the Sageinaga River, and on the Seine and Maligne, there are extensive forests of red and white pine. Occasional white pine appears in the beautiful valley of Rainy River, and on the islands in the Lake of the Woods.

The approach to Fort Frances is very beautiful. As we near the outlet of Rainy Lake, and enter Rainy River, the right bank appears very much like a park, the trees standing far apart, and having the rounded tops of those seen in open grounds. Blue oak and balsam poplar, with a few aspen, are the principal forest trees. These line the bank, and for two miles after leaving the lake, we glide down between walls of living green, until we reach the Fort, which is beautifully situated on the right bank of Rainy River, immediately below the falls. All sorts of grain can be raised here, as well as all kinds of garden vegetables. Barley, three feet high, and oats over that, show there is nothing in the climate or soil to prevent a luxuriant growth. The length of the river is about eighty miles. The right, or Canadian bank, for the whole distance, is covered with a heavy growth of forest trees, shrubs, climbing vines, and beautiful flowers. The forest trees consist of oak, elm, ash, birch, basswood, balsam, spruce, aspen, balsam poplar, and white and red pine near the Lake of the Woods. The whole flora of this region indicates a climate very like that of the old settled parts of Ontario, and the luxuriance of the vegetation shews that the soil is of the very best quality.

The name of Alberton has been given to the settlement at Fort Frances.

Of the lakes in this section, the Lake of the Woods is the most extensive. From Lac Plat, which may be regarded as its western extremity, to White Fish Lake, which is a somewhat similiar extension in an opposite direction, the distance is not far short of 100 miles, and from the mouth of Rainy River, at the entrance of the lake, to its outlet at Rat Portage, in lat 49° 47′ north, and long. 94° 44′ west, the distance is about 70 miles, so that altogether it occupies an area of about sixteen hundred square miles. This extensive sheet of water, like all the other lakes on the line of route, is interspersed with islands, on some of which the Indians have grown maize from time immemorial, and have never known it fail. It would be difficult to conceive anything more beautiful of its kind than the scenery of this lake. Islands rise in continuous clusters, and in every variety of form. Sometimes in passing through them the prospect seems entirely shut in ; soon again it opens out, and through long vistas a glance is obtained of an ocean-like expanse, where the waters meet the horizon.

Geological Features.

From the mouth of Rainy River, for a distance of fifty miles north-wards, the rocks found on the islands of the Lake of the Woods and points of mainland, are principally composed of granite and gneiss. The granite is of a reddish color, and of excellent quality. Quarries are found here easy of access, where blocks can be got of any size, and columns of any length that may be desired.

From the end of Whitefish Bay at Turtle Portage, the formation changes, and from that point to a short distance north of Rat Portage the rocks are of Huronian formation, and are composed largely of argillaceous, silicious, chloritic, dioritic, talcose and green stone slates, schist, trap and hornblende. This formation covers a great part of the islands of the Lake of the Woods, Petamugan Bay and Shoal Lake, and continues in a north-easterly direction across the line of the Canadian Pacific Railway. In this broad belt, at least twenty miles in width, there have been a great number of quartz veins discovered, containing gold and silver, galena, copper and iron pyrites ; several hundred locations have been surveyed, all of which bear indications of gold or silver. In many of these veins, gold can be seen with the naked eye, but it is usually distributed through the rock in fine particles, and can be taken out by grinding and washing.

Rat Portage Water Privileges.

The waters of the Winnipeg River flow out of the Lake of the Woods by two channels through a narrow wall of rocks, with a fall of upward of seventeen feet, and form a bay below, where they unite. Besides the two channels that form the Winnipeg River, there are a number of openings in the rock which have been the beds of rivers at a period when the waters of the lake were higher than they are now. These channels cross the line of the Canadian Pacific Railway, and extend for a distance of upwards of three miles westward from Rat Portage at the most easterly outlet of the lake. They can be opened out and converted into mill races at compara-tively little expense. No dams are required, and no flood can ever break through the embankment to do injury. The power that can be obtained here is unlimited, and the supply of water endless. The value of these water privileges is enhanced by the railway crossing at the very point where mills can be erected adjoining the track. There is no other point on the continent of America possessing water power of such magnitude ; situated so advantageously on the great thoroughfare between the Pacific and Atlantic Oceans, and lying immediately east of the grain-growing region of the western prairie, and on the direct route to a European market.

The more this part of the country is explored, the higher the estimate formed of its value. That it is rich in minerals cannot be questioned ; its forests are of immense value, affording fuel, building timber, railway ties, bridge timber, telegraph poles, fence posts and rails.

Its lakes and rivers abound with a superior quality of fish ; whitefish, sturgeon, lake trout, pickerel, suckers, pike, gold eyes, tuleby, maskinonge, catfish, and perch, which can be shipped to points where the supply is not equal to the demand.

LAKE ABBITIBBE AND THE COUNTRY SOUTH OF IT.

White and red pine are found scattered over the whole region between Lake Temiscaming and Lake Abbitibbe. They are quite abundant and of excellent quality on the slopes of the hills along both sides of the Height of Land. On the hill rising to the height of 700 feet above Lake Mata-wagogig on the north side of the Height of Land, several trees have been measured and found to be from eight to nine feet in circumference, at a height of four or five feet from the ground ; and from the summit of the hill groves of white pine are observed in all directions. White spruce, yellow birch and cedar are also tolerably abundant and of good size. Fine speci-mens of the latter tree, tall and straight, are observed, chiefly in hollows among the hills, on the south side of Lake Abbitibbe.

Sugar maple is tolerably plentiful round the head of Lake Temiscaming, but is not seen further north. The same remark applies to swamp maple and white oak. Large numbers of these grow on low level land near the mouth of the Blanche, and also in smaller quantities at the mouths of other rivers falling into the same lake.

The most abundant tree in this region, north of the limit of sugar maple, is aspen, after which come canoe-birch, spruce, Banksian pine, and Canada balsam. Elm and ash occur occasionally on low flats as far north, as Lake Abbitibbe.

The whole region, extending northward from the mouth of the Montreal River, which is about thirty miles south of the head of Lake Temiscaming, may be correctly described as a level clay plain, with a great number of rocky hills and ridges protruding through it.

The height of the clay appears to be pretty uniform throughout the whole region. Around Lake Abbitibbe it is about thirty feet above the level of the lake, which is estimated to be 245 feet higher than Lake Temiscaming. On the Blanche, the highest clay plains, about thirty-five miles up the river, are about 275 feet above Lake Temiscaming. The Height of Land Portage is about 60 feet above Lake Abbitibbe, or 305 above Temiscaming. Taking the mean of these heights, and adding it to 612 feet, height of Lake Temiscaming above the sea, we find that the height of this clay plain above the sea is about 900 feet.

The largest areas of arable land are on the Blanche, and around Lake Abbitibbe. This lake is surrounded on all sides by level clay land. At a good many points, however, the rock rises above the level of the clay. To the north, and especially to the north-westward, the clay level seems almost unbroken, and it is well known that it extends in this direction to the shores of James' Bay.

Several acres of this clay soil are cultivated at the Hudson's Bay Company's Post at Abbitibbe with satisfactory results, and some of the residents are inclined to insist that all the ordinary cereals can be cultivated as successfully there as on the St. Lawrence.

Indian corn is grown at more than one locality near the head of Lake Temiscaming, and is said to ripen well.

THE TERRITORY NORTH OF THE HEIGHT OF LAND.

Between the Great Lakes and James' Bay the country is of a very different character in each of the two geological areas which it embraces, namely, the Laurentian and Huronian plateau; and the palæozoic and tertiary basin of James' Bay. The former is somewhat elevated, undulating, and dotted with great numbers of lakes; while the latter is low, level, swampy, and, as far as known, generally free from lakes, constituting a well-marked geographical as well as geological basin, bounded by a distinct rim of hard ancient rocks for five-sixths of its circumference, since it contracts to a width of only about 200 miles where it opens into Hudson's Bay on a line between Capes Jones and Henrietta Maria. This rim is high, and has a steep slope to the centre all round.

Owing to the unyielding nature of the rocks, all the rivers running into James' Bay meet with a great and very rapid descent on reaching the edge of this basin. As a consequence, "the long portages" on all of them occur where they pour down this slope. The Long Portage of Rupert's River is close to the bay, while those of Abbitibbe, the Mattagami, and the Missinibi are met with a short distance southward of the margin of the palæozoic rocks. The Kakeami, or principal fall of the Albany, occupies a corresponding position. The Kenogami River, flowing from Long Lake to the Albany, offers a more uniform and gentle descent into this basin than any of the other rivers which have been examined.

Although the Laurentian and Huronian Plateau between the great lakes and James' Bay may be styled a rocky country, still, the proportion of its whole area in which the bare rocks are exposed is much less than is commonly supposed. This opinion is formed after an examination of it in hundreds of places, at a distance from the shores of lakes and rivers, throughout an area of nearly 200,000 square miles between the Ottawa River and Lake Winnipeg. The high and rocky points are naturally more conspicuous in proportion to their horizontal extent than the rest of the country, while the portages, which are almost the only parts seen by ordinary travellers, are nearly always at the most rocky places in the valleys or lower levels. As a matter of experience, in this sort of country, in the District of Algoma and elsewhere, the quantity of cultivatable land on the establishment of settlements, always proves to be much greater than it appeared while in a state of nature.

The banks of the Mattagami and Moose Rivers from the Long Portage to Moose Factory usually consist of brown gravelly earth, underlayed by bluish bouldery clay, and gradually diminish in height, in descending the river, from fifty feet, above high water mark at the foot of the Long Portage, to only about ten at the junction of the Missinibi. The average difference between high and low water mark in the Moose River and its branches, appears to be about ten feet.

The solid rock is not often seen, except under the water in the bed of the stream. Leaving the foot of the Long Portage, the first exposure of solid rock, which is also the principal one on the river, begins at 17 miles, or, at the head of the Grand Rapid, which is about a mile and a quarter long, and has a fall of about twenty feet. The blue clay at the Grand Rapid contains the first marine shells observed on the river. The height above the sea level is in the neighborhood of 300 feet. Lignite, having a bright glossy fracture, is found on the shore at the foot of the rapids.

This locality is also remarkable for the occurrence of a large deposit of iron ore. Its position is on the north-west side of the river, at the foot of the rapids.

Leaving the Grand Rapids, no rock *in situ* is observed until arriving at the " White, or Gypsum Banks," on the Main Moose River. They occur on both sides of the river, and begin at thirty-eight miles above Moose Factory. The gypsum bank on the south-east side runs for about two miles ; that on the opposite side, about half that distance.

The Moose River divides into the Mattagami and Missinibi branches. Fragments of lignite are strewn, often in abundance, along the bed of the river to Coal Brook, where it is seen *in situ,* during very low water. Similar lignite is found on the Albany River.

CLIMATE, AGRICULTURAL RESOURCES, STOCK-RAISING, &c.

Throughout the whole of the region from Lake Nipissing to the Lake of the Woods, the depth of snow is generally less on an average than it is at the City of Ottawa. Only in one locality between these two points is the snow found generally so deep as at this city, namely, in the immediate neighborhood of Lake Superior, where the lake appears to have a local influence on the humidity of the atmosphere, and, in consequence, on the amount of snow-fall.

The climate of the territory north of the Height of Land is one of extremes. The winters are cold—the temperature falling sometimes as low as forty degrees below zero of Fahrenheit's thermometer, and occasionally rising in summer to ninety degrees in the shade on the coast of James' Bay. The mean temperature of the summer at Moose Factory is about sixty degrees.

In going northward, from the Height of Land towards James' Bay, the climate does not appear to get worse, but rather better. This may be due to the constant diminution in the elevation, more than counterbalancing for the increased latitude, since in these northern regions a change in alti-

3

tude affects the climate much more than the same amount of change would affect it in places further south. The water of James' Bay may also exert a favourable influence, the bulk of it being made up in the summer time, of warm river water, which accumulates in the head of the bay, and pushes the cold sea-water further north. The greater proportion of day to night during the summer months may be another cause of the comparative warmth of this region.

The rain-fall at Moose Factory forms no criterion as to what it is on the southern highlands, where, without being too wet, there is sufficient rain and dew to support the most luxuriant vegetation. The snow-fall at Moose Factory is not nearly as heavy as it is south of Lake Nipissing and the French River.

The following tables of temperature and rain-fall at Prince Arthur's Landing and Moose Factory are taken from the Report of the Meteorological service of Canada, for the year ending 31st December, 1881.

PRINCE ARTHUR'S LANDING.

1881.	January.	February.	March.	April.	May.	June.	July.	August.	September.	October.	November.	December.
Mean temperature of the several months.	0·5	10·7	25·8	34·2	50·4	56·5	67·1	64·4	53·7	40·6	22·9	21·2
Highest temperature in each month.	29·8	38·4	45·5	71·8	70·8	80·7	88·6	85·6	72·3	69·8	49·8	42·5
Lowest temperature in each month.	−36·6	−25·4	−12·0	3·1	20·2	29·5	43·2	38·0	33·0	15·3	−13·3	−19·4
Rainfall in inches in each month.	0·00	0·00	0·00	0·76	3·23	1·74	2·71	2·97	7·38	2·66	1·00	0·00
Number of days on which rain fell in each month.	0	0	0	3	10	8	8	6	15	5	2	0

MOOSE FACTORY.

1881.	January.	February.	March.	April.	May.	June.	July.	August.	September.	October.	November.	December.
Mean temperature of the several months.	−10·6	6·9	16·1	22·6	48·2	47·4	64·0	60·8	51·5	32·6	12·3	8·0
Highest temperature in each month.	20·1	36·1	44·2	56·8	79·0	83·0	90·5	88·5	76·8	71·2	52·0	37·1
Lowest temperature in each month.	−39·6	−34.5	−14·3	17·9	14·0	26·8	41.5	38.2	35·0	12.5	−29·1	−22·2
Rainfall in inches in each month.	0·00	0·20	0·10	0·16	0·52	3·53	2·35	2·82	4.80	1·52	0·90	0·00
Number of days on which rain fell in each month.	0	1	2	5	11	14	16	13	17	5	1	0

RESULTS of Meteorological Observations at Moose

	1877.					
	November.	December.	January.	February.	March.	April.
Mean temperature	29°.0	20°.7	1°.1	13°.3	20°.4	35°.6
Highest temperature	41·0	38·4	32·7	42·5	48·1	66·1
Lowest temperature	8·0	9·8	35·9	21·7	22·4	8·9
Monthly range	36·0	48·2	68·6	64·2	70·5	57·2
Mean daily range	11·1	13·3	19·8	20·9	21·0	16·6
Mean temperature of warmest day.	40·0	36·1	30·0	36·8	37·6	61·2
Mean temperature of coldest day	16·3	1·3	26·7	7·7	1·0	23·7
Amount of rain in inches	0·85	0·29	R	0·00	0·04	1·22
Greatest fall in one day	0·35	0·29			0.04	0.37
Number of days' rain	5	1	1	0	1	6
Amount of snow	0·8	0·5	0·3	0·2	0·8	0·1
Greatest fall in one day	0·3	0·2	0·2	0·2	0·2	0·1
Number of days' snow	6	9	9	5	15	2
Number of fair days	19	21	22	23	16	22
Percentage of cloud	73	80	53	47	61	65

Factory, compiled at the Meteorological Office, Toronto.

	1878.								1879.					
May.	June.	July.	August.	September.	October.	November.	December.	January.	February.	March.	April.	May.	June.	July.
47°.3	57°.0	66°.9	63°.0	51°.7	40°.9	26°.5	7°.6	3°.9	6°.7	12°.1	24°.2	39°.9	50°.2	60°.3
76·5	92·1	91·6	81·3	73·9	66·8	40·8	32·9	24·0	19·1	46·3	52·2	73·3	81·7	84·8
19·1	26·9	41·8	34·9	31·1	7·6	4·3	18·4	40·3	41·3	33·4	7·0	22·2	27·0	35·7
57·4	65·2	49·8	46·4	42·8	59.2	36·5	51·3	64·3	60·4	79·7	59·2	51·1	54·7	59·1
16·4	20·3	21·2	16·8	17·6	15·6	11·0	13·2	19·4	21·2	26·0	14·6	19·9	19·0	21·6
73·5	88·1	84·2	74·9	68·0	63·4	38·1	28·4	20·6	16·5	39·5	44·2	59·9	70·8	76·2
23·1	32·4	52·4	50·8	40·2	21·2	11·8	11·5	28·2	30·6	10·7	1·0	28·5	34·2	42·6
1·95	1·64	2·79	6·11	5·46	1·74	R	R	0·0	0·0	0·60	1·00	2·08	3·47	5·42
0·41	0·56	1·33	1·23	1·06	0·51	.....	.....	.....	.....	0·30	0·75	1·10	0·87	2·12
11	9	12	17	19	14	3	1	0	0	3	5	7	16	18
0·8	S	.....	.....	.....	3·0	25·5	27·4	9·6	8·1	9·8	15·8	2·0	5·0	.....
0·7	.....	.....	.....	.....	3·0	7·0	4·0	2·0	2·0	4·0	7·0	1·0	4·7	.....
4	1	.....	.....	.....	5	19	23	16	10	13	12	5	3	.....
17	21	18	14	11	12	9	7	15	18	15	13	20	12	13
76	63	59	70	75	71	79	78	61	55	63	69	67	68	56

TABLES shewing the Monthly Mean Temperature (Farnh. Therm.) for two years, at the Hudson Bay Company's Post on Lake Temiscaming, Lat. 47° 19' North; Long. 79° 31' West; 630 feet above the level of the sea.—From a Register kept by Mr. Severight.

1843-4.

Month.	Sunrise.	Noon.	Sunset.	Mean for each month.	Clear sunshine.	Clear and cloudy.	Cloudy.	Cloudy and rain.	Cloudy and snow.
1843.									
November.........	24 5/30	29 6/30	27	26 2/3	3	10	5	2	10
December.........	18 26/31	26 5/31	22 25/31	22 1/2	2	10	13	1	5
1844.									
January..	-1 12/31	12 24/31	10 2/31	7 1/6	13	5	6	....	7
February..........	8 24/29	28 6/29	19 22/29	19	7	9	6	....	7
March.............	13 18/31	33	25 10/31	23 1/3	14	8	5	....	4
April	33 17/30	53 23/30	45 2/30	44	23	1	2	4	....
May..............	42 4/31	57 14/31	50 14/31	50	12	8	....	11	....
June	56 2/30	70 22/30	61 6/30	62 2/3	11	4	3	12	....
July..............	58 5/31	72 11/31	66 15/31	65 2/3	9	8	3	11	....
August...........	56 26/31	71 9/31	63 25/31	64	10	6	....	15	....
September.........	48	63 15/30	56 15/30	56	13	7	1	9	....
October	34 6/31	46	42 9/31	40 5/6	11	8	1	5	6

1844-5.

Month.	Sunrise.	Noon.	Sunset.	Mean for each month.	Clear sunshine.	Clear and cloudy.	Cloudy.	Cloudy and rain.	Cloudy and snow.
1844.									
November	24 16/30	31 4/30	28 4/30	28	4	7	8	3	8
December..........	11 23/31	19 14/31	16 8/31	15 5/6	9	8	8	....	6
1845.									
January...........	8 19/31	17 23/31	13 18/31	13 1/3	6	15	3	1	6
February.....	11 15/28	24 25/28	20 4/28	18 5/6	7	8	5	3	5
March.............	19	34 25/31	28 20/31	27 1/2	9	10	3	2	7
April	26 19/30	43 16/30	36	35 1/3	5	11	....	8	6
May..............	38 16/31	56	49	47 5/6	13	7	5	6	....
June	51 18/30	69 25/30	62 6/30	61 1/6	12	7	5	6	....
July.............	58	75 7/31	67 27/31	67	8	12	....	11	....
August	58	76 16/31	67 9/31	67 1/3	15	10	....	6	....
September	48 7/30	58 5/30	53 14/30	53 1/3	1	8	2	19	....
October	38	50	46	44 2/3	11	10	3	7	....

Agricultural operations have been very limited north of the Height of Land. It is only at the fur-trading posts of the Hudson's Bay Company that any attempt has been made to cultivate the soil.

Farming and gardening have been successfully carried on by the officers of the Company at their posts on Lakes Mattagami and Missinibi. At the latter, spring wheat has been found to ripen well. At Moose Factory, although the soil is a cold, wet clay, with a level, undrained surface, farm and garden produce, in considerable variety, are raised every year. Oats, barley, beans, peas, turnips, beets, carrots, cabbage, onions, tomatoes, &c., are grown without any more care than is required in other parts of Canada.

Wheat may be successfully grown where the soil is suitable in all that part of this territory lying to the south of the fiftieth parallel of latitude. The mean temperature of the summer south of that parallel is sufficient to ripen this cereal. Indeed wheat has been grown at Abbitibbe House, Flying Post, and New Brunswick, on or about the forty-ninth parallel, and at Lac Seul, between the fiftieth and fifty-first parallel. Indian corn, a more delicate plant than wheat, has come to maturity at Osnaburgh House. on Lake St. Joseph, north of the fifty-first parallel.

Barley, oats, rye, peas and beans succeed well. The invariable excellence of the crops of the Windsor bean and the kidney-bean at Moose Factory is surprising.

The vetch grows wild everywhere, but nowhere is it so abundant as on the coast of James' Bay.

There is probably no food plant that is likely to be of more importance to the inhabitants of this territory than the potato. There is none the cultivation of which has been so successful in every part. The fitness both of soil and climate for its growth has been established beyond dispute. Whether viewed in reference to size, quantity or quality, the crops at Moose Factory and Matawagamingue (260 miles further south), will compare favourably with those in the best potato-growing districts in Ontario. Peaty soil is particularly well suited to the growth of potatoes. There are millions of acres of peat mosses in this territory, very extensive areas of which can be easily reclaimed, and when the country is settled and means of transport provided, hundreds of thousands of tons of potatoes may be grown and sent away to supply the wants of other countries.

The fitness of the soil and climate for the growth of root crops will make the breeding of cattle and dairy husbandry important resources of this territory. Among these crops the turnip is entitled to a place in the front rank. The carrot, beet, and parsnip can also be grown.

Cabbages, spinach, lettuce, mustard, cress, and radishes are grown without any difficulty. Rhubarb also grows well. The cauliflower appears to be one of the surest crops at Moose Factory, and is sometimes ready for the table as early as the first of August.

Whatever doubts exist as to the agricultural value of the country north of the Height of Land in respect to its grain-growing capabilities, there can be none in regard to its fitness to produce the more important roots and grasses, From the Height of Land northward to the coast of James' Bay, nothing on the north shores of Lake Huron or Superior can exceed the luxuriance of the native grasses. Cows and oxen are kept at all the principal Posts, and they are invariably found to be healthy and in fine condition ; a good evidence of the salubrity of the climate, and excellence of the pasture. At Moose Factory where some sixty head are constantly kept, a certain number are slaughtered every Fall, and are quite fat, although then taken straight from the grass.

The only fruits that appear to be cultivated in the garden are the red and black currant and raspberry. The red currant is remarkably prolific. The strawberry and goosberry might be raised with little trouble, for they are found growing wild in many places, and nowhere more plentifully or of finer quality than on the coast. The huckleberry, or blueberry is found in great profusion from the long portages to the Height of Land. Indeed ' it may be said to abound from the coast of Hudson's Bay to the shores of Lakes Huron and Superior. It is nowhere in greater profusion or of finer quality than on the Height of Land itself.

There is another wild fruit which may be noticed. This is a bush or tree not unlike the wild cherry in appearance.* North of the Height of Land, it attains a height in some places of ten or twelve feet, but is generally about six feet. The fruit grows singly, not in bunches or clusters on the tree. It is an oblong or pear shape, larger than the blueberry, but smaller than the grape. When ripe it is of a purple or blue color, It is sweeter and has more flavor than the huckleberry, and is preferred by the natives to it. It is to be found all the way from James' Bay to Lake Huron, but nowhere in greater perfection than on the Mattagami River. The fruit is not only pleasant and wholesome, but the juice would make an excellent wine, and the tree is worthy of cultivation and a place in our orchards and gardens.

---

* This is probably Amelanchier Sanguinea, a variety of the Canadian Medlar.

GENERAL ACCOUNT OF HUDSON'S AND JAMES' BAY.

The southern and western shores of James' Bay are very low and level, and the bay itself is remarkably shallow, with the exception of a channel down its centre. For long distances it is only possible to land from a small boat at high tide. Between high tide mark and the woods there is generally a broad, open or marshy belt interspersed with clumps of willow bushes, and divided by muddy creeks. , In some places this open border is raised above all but the highest spring tides, and constitutes a level prairie, supporting a rich growth of grasses and sedges. The marshy outline of the shore of the bay is often interrupted by points and peninsula-like islands, composed of boulders piled together in thousands with scarcely any finer materials amongst them.

Owing to the numerous large rivers flowing into the southern portion of James' Bay, the water of this part is only brackish, and in some instances no taste of salt can be perceived for miles, even at a considerable distance from the land. It is so shallow that a person may frequently touch the bottom with an oar, when almost out of sight of the low shore in a boat. The constant currents kept up by the ebbing and flowing of the tides over this shallow, muddy bottom, render the water too turbid for fish to live in this part of the bay, although they exist in the clearer water further out.

In the popular mind Hudson's Bay is apt to be associated with the polar regions; yet no part of it comes within the Arctic Circle, and the latitude of its southern extremity is south of London. Few people have any adequate conception of the extent of this great Canadian Sea. Including its southern prolongation, James' Bay, it measures about one thousand miles in length, and is more than six hundred miles in width in its northern part. Its total area is in the neighborhood of 500,000 square miles, or upwards of half that of the Mediterranean.

The resources of Hudson's Bay and the country immediately around it are varied and numerous, although, as yet, few of them are at all developed. The fur trade is the principal and best known business which has hitherto been carried on in these regions; but a considerable amount of oil, derived from the larger whales, the porpoises, walruses, white bears, and various species of seals which frequent the northern part of the bay, has been carried to New England, and small quantities, principally of porpoise and seal oil, have from time to time been taken to London by the Hudson's Bay Company. The trade in oil might be greatly extended in these quarters. Other articles have been exported from the bay, but hitherto only in trifling quantities. They embrace whalebone, feathers, quills, castoreum, lead ore, sawn lumber, ivory, tallow, isinglass, and skins of seals and porpoises. The fisheries, properly speaking, of Hudson's Bay, have not been investigated. Both the Indians and Eskimo find a variety of fish for their own use, and fine salmon abound in the rivers of Hudson's Strait. Water fowl are very numerous on both sides of the bay.

But perhaps the most important of the undeveloped resources of the country around the bay are its soil, timber and minerals. To the south and south-west of James' Bay, in the latitude of Devonshire and Cornwall, there is a large tract in which much of the land is good, and the climate sufficiently favourable for the successful prosecution of stock and dairy farming.

Some of the timber found in the country which sends its waters into James' Bay may prove to be of value for export. Among the kinds which it produces may be mentioned white, red and pitch pine, black and white spruce, balsam, larch, white cedar, and white birch. The numerous rivers which converge towards the head of James' Bay offer facilities for "driving" timber to points at which it may be shipped by sea-going vessels

In view of the completion of the railway from Lake Nipissing to James Bay, minerals may become in future the greatest of the resources of Hudson's Bay. Little direct search has been made for the valuable minerals of these regions. A large deposit of rich ironstone has been found on the Mattagami River. In 1877 inexhaustible supplies of good manganiferous iron ore were discovered on the islands near the Eastmain coast, and promising quantities of galena around Richmond Gulf, and also near Little Whale River. Traces of gold, silver, molybdenum, and copper have also been found on the Eastmain coast. Lignite is met with on the Missinibi gypsum on the Moose, and petroleum-bearing limestone on the Abbitibbe River. Soapstone is abundant not far from Musquito Bay on the east side, and iron pyrites between Churchill and Marble Island on the west. Good building stones, clays and limestones exist on both sides of the bay. A cargo of mica is said to have been taken from Chesterfield Inlet to New York, and valuable deposits of plumbago are reported to occur on the north side of Hudson's Strait.

WILD ANIMALS AND GAME.

Cariboo range all through the territory, either singly or in small parties of eight or ten. The moose are becoming very scarce in the region west and north of Lake Superior, although still plentiful north of Lake Nipissing. Black bears are found everywhere. In the vicinity of James' Bay and Hudson's Bay there is a bear, dark brown in color, and in form halfway between the common black and polar bear. Wolves are scarce, as also are their chief prey, the red deer. The lynx is frequently met with, and so too is the thievish and mischievous wolverine.

The rabbit, or rather hare, is ubiquitous here as elsewhere. The common brown, and the more rare and very beautiful silver fox, are among the denizens of this territory. The black fox, a beautiful creature with silky hair, is now and then seen and captured.

Beaver abound in the streams and creeks. The otter, fisher, and mink are plentiful; while, in the more northern regions, the marten attains a high degree of beauty and corresponding value. The musk-rat builds his dwelling on the banks of the rivers. The beaver and musk-rat are both good eating. The ermine is of a brown color in summer, but in winter becomes perfectly white, with a black tip on its tail, in which condition it is most valuable for marketable purposes. The opossum is a native of the territory, and the porcupine is occasionally found. The common red squirrel abounds, and there are a great many large squirrels of different colors. Of the skunk, and other representatives of the weasel tribe, there are varieties enough.

Of feathered game, wild fowl of all kinds are exceedingly abundant, and are killed in great numbers in the Spring and Fall, more particularly the Fall. At this time vast numbers of wild geese, ducks, teal, plover and snipe, gather on the coast of James' Bay, and remain several weeks before migrating to the south.

Partridge, fantail grouse, and willow grouse, are extremely plentiful.

The feathers of the wild goose, and the down of the wild swan, have long been articles of trade by the Hudson's Bay Company.

CANADIAN PACIFIC RAILWAY.

It requires no prophetic eye to see that the construction of the Canadian Pacific Railway will change the face of this country, and develop its agricultural and mineral resources.

With these objects steadily in view, the Commissioner of Crown Lands has caused tiers of Townships to be surveyed along the route from Callander to Sudbury Junction, and thence to Algoma Mills; and others will be surveyed between Sudbury and the Pic River as construction advances between these points.

Commencing at North Bay on Lake Nipissing, the names of the Townships which have been surveyed along the line are as follows:—

Widdifield, Springer, Field, Badgerow, Caldwell, Kirkpatrick, Hugel, Ratter, Dunnet, Hagar, Awrey, Dryden, Neelon, McKim, Snider, Waters, Graham, Nairn, Merritt, Hallam, May, Salter, Victoria, Shedden, Lewis, Spragge, Esten, Long, Striker, Mack, Scarfe, and Cobden.

It is stated by the authorities of the Canadian Pacific Railway that eight millions of acres have been found fit for settlement between Callander and the Michipicoten valley.

In this broad field, centres of business activity are springing up along the line, notably at north Bay, Sturgeon Falls, Sudbury, Spanish River and Algoma Mills.

Algoma Mills, the Lake Huron terminus of the branch of the Canadian Pacific Railway which diverges from the main line at Sudbury Junction, is destined to become an important place. From its natural advantages it was selected by the Company as the port from which their Lake Superior steamers should ply, and they are erecting a handsome summer hotel there, which is intended not only for the accommodation of the travelling public, but especially designed for the comfort of summer pleasure-seekers, who will undoubtedly be attracted to this delightful spot, until now so little known.

For the accommodation of immigrants, a comfortable house is being built, in which, while waiting for the steamer, they may rest and have their meals.

To provide for the handling of the grain in transit from the North-West, a large elevator is being built at Algoma (there being one at Port Arthur also), and by this means, through shipment to Europe by way of Montreal will be greatly facilitated, the distance being considerably less than by any other route. It stands to reason, therefore, that the works referred to, together with the repair shops, etc., necessary to a railway terminus, will entail a permanent settlement of no inconsiderable proportions.

The fleet of steamers built on the Clyde by the Canadian Pacific Railway Company consists of the " Algoma," " Alberta," and " Athabasca."

They are 275 feet long, constructed of steel, built in water tight compartments, and their design covers all the latest improvements in marine architecture best adapted for Lake Superior navigation.

Eighty miles east of Sudbury Junction is North Bay, on the north shore of charming Lake Nipissing. ˙This being a divisional point of the Canadian Pacific Railway, it is the headquarters of a large number of men ; and an extensive repair shop, round house, etc., have already been erected there.

On the shores of the lake, and amongst its islands, are many picturesque sites, which, from present indications, will soon be occupied by summer homes of residents of Ottawa and Montreal.

Stations of the Canadian Pacific Railway.

NORTH BAY, in the Township of Widdifield.

BEAUCAGE, in the Indian Reserve.

MEDOWSIDE, in the Indian Reserve.

STURGEON FALLS, in the Township of Springer.

VERNER, in the Township of Springer.

BURNSIDE, in the Township of Caldwell.

VEUVE, in the Township of Dunnet.

MARKSTAY, in the Township of Hagar.

WAHNAPITAE, in the Township of Dryden.

ROMFORD, in the Township of Neelon.

SUDBURY JUNCTION, in the Township of KcMim.

OTHER SURVEYS AND CROWN LAND AGENCIES.

The following Townships have been surveyed on the Mississaga. Thessalon, Echo and Garden Rivers, and their tributaries :—Thompson, Patton, Bright, and Bright Additional, Gladstone, Parkinson, Day, Wells, Thessalon (Indian), Kirkwood, Bridgland, Haughton, Lefroy, Rose, Galbraith, Plummer, and Plummer Additional, Tarbutt, and Tarbutt Additional, Johnson, Coffin, and Coffin Additional. Chesley, and Chesley Additional, McMahon, Gillmor and Whitman.

In this section, there is a Crown Land Agency at Bruce Mines.

Here, neat farm houses, surrounded with barns and stables, with full garners, and social hearths ; and fields of wheat, barley, peas, oats and potatoes, remind us of the older settled portions of the Province.

The Townships of Laird, Meredith, and McDonald have been surveyed in the Garden River Indian Reserve.

North of the Town of Sault Ste. Marie, and in the neighbourhood of Goulais Bay, and Batchawaung Bay, are the Townships of St. Mary, Tarentorus, Korah, Awenge, Parke, Prince, Dennis, Pennefather, Aweres, Jarvis, Anderson, Hodgins, Deroche, Vankoughnet, Fenwick, Kars, Ley, Haviland, Tupper, Archibald, Tilly, Fisher, Herrick, Palmer, and Ryan.

In this section, there is a Crown Land Agency at Sault Ste. Marie.

North and west of Lake Superior, there are the Townships of Pic, Neepigon, Dorion, Lyon, McTavish, Macgregor, Sibley, McIntyre, Neebing, Paipoonge, Blake, Crooks, Pardee, Oliver and Moss.

There is a Crown Land Agency at Port Arthur, on Thunder Bay.

SYSTEMS OF SURVEY.

On the North shores of Lakes Huron and Superior some townships have been laid out on following system.

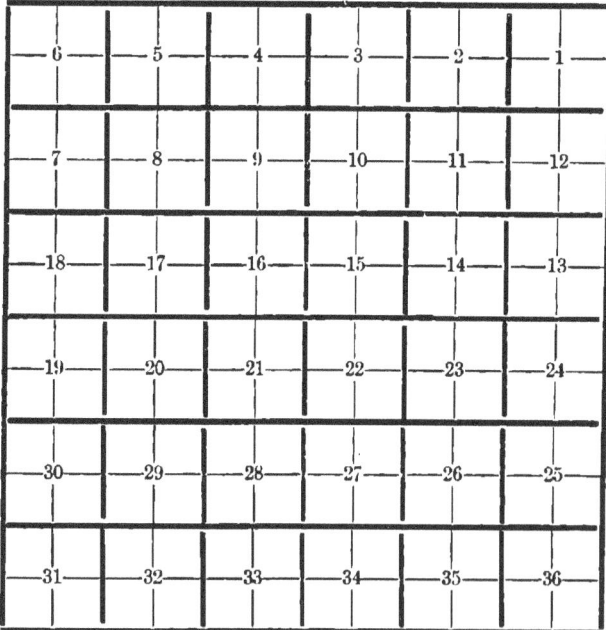

This Diagram exhibits the thirty-six sections of a township.

The country to be surveyed is first divided by meridians, six miles distant from each other, and then again by a system of East and West lines also six miles from each other. The country is thus divided into equal squares which are called townships. Each township is a square six miles on a side, and contains thirty-six square miles.

It is subdivided into thirty-six sections of six hundred and forty acres, or one square mile each, and they are numbered from the north-east angle. There are no road allowances staked off on the ground, but five per cent. of the area is reserved for roads.

A modification or variation of this system is, however, now generally adopted in the new townships of these districts, in which the old and familiar names of "lots and concessions" have been retained, while the outlines of the township remain the same. The lots are divided so as to contain three hundred and twenty acres, or half a section each, and like the section townships, no road allowances are staked off, but five per cent. of the area is reserved for roads in the patents.

This last Diagram will illustrate it.

					VI.						
					V.						
12	11	10	9	8	IV. 7	6	5	4	3	2	1
					III.						
					II.						
					I.						

Land is commonly measured with a chain called Gunter's Chain. It is

4 poles, or 22 yards, or 66 feet long, and composed of 100 equal parts called links, each link being $7\frac{92}{100}$ inches. An acre consists of 10 square chains, or 100,000 square links. A statute pole, perch, or rod is $16\frac{1}{2}$ feet long. There are 80 chains in a mile and 640 acres in a square mile.

ECONOMIC MINERALS.

IRON, Specular Iron Ore.—*Lake Huron*, Wallace Mine location, near White Fish River, (a 15 feet vein); Desert Lake, near Bruce Mines, Killarney.

Lake Superior.—Batchewaung Bay, Gros Cap, Michipicoten, Loon Lake on Thunder Bay, Pic River, Magpie River.

Lake Nipissing.—Iron Island.

MAGNETIC IRON ORE.—North shore of Lake Superior.

COPPER, Sulphurets, etc.—*Lake Superior*, Spar Island, Prince's location, a four feet vein, (vitreous sulphuret with silver); St. Ignace Island (native copper with silver), Michipicoten Island (native copper with silver), Michipicoten Bay, Mica Bay, Mamainse (yellow, variegated and vitreous sulphurets), Battle Island, Cape Gargantua, Batchewaung Bay, Pointe aux Mines, Mica Bay, Black River, Black Bay, Thunder Bay.

Lake Huron.—Root River (yellow sulphuret), Bruce Mines (yellow, variegated and vitreous sulphurets), Wallace mine, White Fish River (yellow sulphuret), Echo Lake.

SILVER, native, etc.—*Lake Superior*, St. Ignance, and Michipicoten Islands (native silver with native copper), Prince's location (native silver with sulphuret of silver), Silver Islet near Thunder Cape, Shebandowan District, Rabbit Mountain, south-west of Paipoonge, and many other localities.

GOLD, native in vein.—*Lake Superior*, Prince's location (traces), Shebandowan Lake, Jack-fish Lake, Long Island in Lake of the Woods, Rat Portage.

GALENA.—In mineral veins on north shore of Lake Superior, Prince's location, Thunder Bay and Thunder Cape, Black Bay and Hudson's Bay.

ARGENTIFEROUS GALENA.—On Lake Temiscaming.

BISMUTH.—Near Echo Lake.

NICKEL.—*Lake Huron*, Wallace mine. *Lake Superior*, Michipicoten Island.

LEAD.—At Silver Lake, Thunder Bay, vein of quartz and barytes holding galena ; Enterprise mine, Lake Superior ; Pointe aux mines, Lake Superior, Pigeon River, Kaministiquia River.

BARYTES, Permanent White.—*Lake Superior*, in a multitude of veins on the North shore from Pigeon River to Thunder Cape.

JASPER.—North-west shore of Lake Huron, Batchewaung Bay, and north of Thunder Bay.

AGATES.—*Lake Superior*, St. Ignace and neighbouring islands, Michipicoten Island, and other localities.

AMETHYSTS.—*Lake Superior*, Spar Island, and sundry places along the neighbouring coast.

RIBBOND CHERT (for Cameos.)—*Lake Superior*, on Thunder Bay.

COBALT (for glass staining, and porcelain painting, etc.)—At Prince's mine, Lake Superior (arseniate of cobalt).

Lake Huron.—Wallace mine (traces).

RETINITE, PITCHSTONE, AND BASALT (for making Black Glass).—*Lake Superior*, north shore and islands, Michipicoten Island and East Coast.

Lake Huron.—In the trap dykes of the north shore and neighbouring islands.

WHITE QUARTZ SAND STONE (for making glass).—*Lake Huron*, on the north shore, and the islands near, in great abundance.

STEATITE OR SOAPSTONE.—Near Thunder Bay, and on Hudson's Bay.

ALUM.—On Slate River, a tributary of the Kaministiquia.

FLAGGING STONES.—On Lake Temiscaming.

ROOFING SLATES.—On the Montreal River.

MANGANESE.—Batchewaung Bay on Lake Superior.

MOLYBDENUM (for dyeing purposes, and calico printing).—Terrace Cove on Lake Superior.

ARSENIC.—Several localities on Lake Superior.

ASBESTOS.—West of Sturgeon River, north of the Township of Hagar.

LIGNITE.—On the Missinibi, a branch of the Moose River, and on the Albany River.

GYPSUM.—On the Moose River.

APPENDIX.

DEPARTMENT OF CROWN LANDS,
Toronto, 1st August, 1883.

The following information is communicated in reference to the manner of acquiring title to Public Lands in this Province under the Free Grants and Homesteads Act.

FREE GRANTS AND HOMESTEADS.

1. By the "Free Grants and Homesteads Act," Chapter 25 of the Revised Statutes of Ontario, Public Lands which have been surveyed, and are considered suitable for settlement and cultivation, and not valuable chiefly for minerals or pine timber, may be appropriated as Free Grants ; but such appropriations are to be confined to lands within the Districts of Algoma and Nipissing, and that tract of territory lying between the Ottawa River and Georgian Bay, and comprising the northerly portions of the Counties of Renfrew, Frontenac, Addington, Hastings, Peterborough, Victoria and Simcoe, and the Districts of Muskoka and Parry Sound.

2. To obtain a Free Grant, the applicant must make application to the local Crown Land Agent, in whose agency the land desired is situated, and deposit with him the necessary affidavits. Although no fees are charged by the Department, or allowed to the land agents for locating, yet if required to prepare the necessary affidavits, the agent may make a reasonable charge for so doing.

3. Two hundred acres is the limit of the Act, therefore no individual can obtain more than that quantity as a Free Grant, and if the land selected exceeds the 200 acres, the applicant must pay for the overplus at the price fixed by the Regulations. *A single man over eighteen years of age, or a married man without children under eighteen residing with him, is entitled to a grant of 100 acres.* But in case it shall be shown by satisfactory evidence that a considerable proportion of the land selected by an applicant who comes under either of these headings, cannot be made available for farming purposes on account of rock, swamp or lake, the Commissioner of

Crown Lands may make an allowance for such waste land, and may increase the quantity of land located to such applicant to any number of acres not exceeding in the whole 200 acres. *The male head of a family, or the sole female head of a family, having a child or children under eighteen years of age residing with him or her, may be located for 200 acres as a Free Grant ; and may also purchase an additional 100 acres at the rate of fifty cents per acre, cash.*

In certain townships, however, situated in the Districts of Algoma and Thunder Bay and which are subdivided into sections and quarter sections, or into lots containing 160 or 320 acres each, the locatee, whether he be a single man over eighteen, or the head of a family with children, is entitled to 160 acres only ; that is, a full quarter section, or a half lot, as the case may be ; and he may purchase an additional 160 acres at the rate of fifty cents per acre, cash.

Upon receipt of the necessary affidavits, the agent will, if the land selected be open for location, and there be no adverse claim thereto, enter the locatee for it on the records of his office, and at the end of the current month he will return the location to the Department of Crown Lands.

In case a party has settled on Government land before the township has been surveyed, or appropriated under the Free Grants Act, he should, immediately after it is opened for location, apply to the local agent and get located, as he will have no recognized title, and his occupation of the land will not count until this action has been taken.

4. Upon completion of his location, the locatee may enter upon and occupy his land, and may commence his improvements ; and the Regulations require him to do so within one month.

5. The locatee will not be entitled to his patent until the expiration of five years from the date of location, and he must then make proof that the settlement duties have been fully completed. The settlement duties required on each location are as follows, viz :—

(1) To have at least fifteen acres cleared and had under cultivation, of which two acres at least are to be cleared and cultivated annually during the five years ;

(2) To have built a habitable house, at least 16 by 20 feet in size ;

(3) And to have actually and continuously resided upon and cultivated the land for five years after location.

A locatee is not bound to remain on the land all the time during the five years ; but may be absent on business or at work for, in all, not more than six months in any one year. He must, however, make it his home, and clear and cultivate the quantity of land required (two acres at least) each year.

Where a locatee holds two lots (200 acres) he may make the requisite improvements on either one or both, as he finds it most convenient.

A locatee who purchases an additional 100 acres under the Regulations must, within five years from the date of sale, clear fifteen acres thereon, and cultivate the same, before he will be entitled to the patent ; but he is not required to build a house or reside on the purchased lot, where he holds it in connection with a Free Grant.

The proof of the performance of the settlement duties must be : the affidavit of the locatee himself, supported by the testimony of at least two disinterested parties, which affidavits are to be filed with the local agent,— who, if satisfied as to the correctness of the statements contained therein, recommends the issue of the patent, and transmits the application to the Department.

6. In case the locatee fails to perform the settlement duties required by law, his location is liable to forfeiture, and may be cancelled by the Commissioner of Crown Lands. Applications for cancellation must be made through the local agent, and be supported by the affidavits of the applicant and at least two credible witnesses, who will show what the present position of the lot is : whether the locatee ever occupied or improved, and, if so, to what extent, and the value of the improvements ; when he ceased to occupy ; and his address, if known. Upon receipt of this evidence the agent will, if he can ascertain the address of the locatee, notify him of the application, and call upon him to disprove the allegations, or show cause why his location should not be cancelled, within thirty days. At the expiration of that time the agent will transmit the evidence, with anything he may have received from the locatee in reply, and his own report to the Department.

7. The assignment or mortgage of a homestead from a locatee to another party before the issue of his patent is invalid, and cannot be recognized by the Department. This does not, however, apply to the devise of a Free Grant lot by will, nor to transfers of land by a locatee for church, cemetery or school purposes, or the right of way of railroads.

8. All pine trees and minerals on land located or sold under the Free Grants Act are reserved from the location or sale, and are the property of the Crown ; and the Commissioner of Crown Lands may at any time issue a license to cut the pine on such land. The locatee may, however, cut and

use such pine trees as he requires for building and fencing on his land, and may also cut and dispose of any pine trees he meets with in the actual process of clearing his land for cultivation ; but any trees so disposed of are subject to the payment of the same dues as are payable by license-holders.

Holders of timber licenses have the right to haul their timber over the uncleared portion of any land located or sold, and to make such roads as may be necessary for the purpose, and to use all slides, portages and roads, and to have free access to all streams and lakes.

9. The Crown reserves the right to construct on any land located or sold, any Colonization Road, or deviation from the Government allowance for road ; and to take from such land, without compensation, any timber, gravel or material required for the construction or improvement of any such road.

10. Any conveyance, mortgage or alienation (except a will) of the land located, by a locatee after the issue of patent, and within twenty years from location, will be invalid unless it be by deed in which his wife is one of the grantors, and unless it be duly executed by her.

11. The land while owned by the locatee, his widow or heirs, shall be exempt from liability for debt during twenty years from the date of location. This exemption does not, however, extend to a sale for taxes legally imposed.

12. Where a Free Grant locatee dies before the completion of his title, the widow, devisee or heirs, may continue the settlement duties and obtain a patent at the proper time, upon filing the requisite proof. If the locatee made a will, it should be forwarded to the Department, with evidence showing the time of his death ; and, if married, the name of his widow. In case he made no will, the fact must be shown by evidence, and also the time of his death ; if married, the name of his widow, and the names and ages, residences and occupation of all the children he left, must be set out in full. If he left no widow or children, the name, place of residence, and occupation of his heir or next of kin must be given.

Where a locatee dies, whether before or after issue of patent, leaving a widow, she is entitled to the land during her widowhood in lieu of dower, unless she prefers to take her dower instead.

13. In making application for land, and in filing proof in support of applications for cancellation of a location, or for issue of patent, the applicant will save time and unnecessary trouble by filing his papers with, or mailing them to, the Crown Land Agent in whose agency the land is situated, as on account of the agent's local knowledge of the lands he has

to deal with, the Department requires that his certificate be attached to all such applications.

14 Lands located or sold under the Free Grants and Homesteads Act, or the regulations made thereunder, are liable to taxation from the date of such location or sale, and where taxes, assessed on such lands, are in arrears for three years, the interest of the locatee or purchaser may be sold in the manner prescribed by law. When the tax-purchaser receives his deed, unless legal proceedings be taken to question it by some person interested within two years from the date of sale, he acquires the right and interest of the locatee or purchaser, and may obtain a patent on completion of the original conditions of location or sale.

In order to have his claim recognized, a tax-purchaser should file his deed in the Department, and two years after the date of sale for taxes, should file evidence showing that no action has been taken to question his title, that there is no adverse claim on the ground of occupation or improvements, and that all arrears of taxes have been paid since he purchased. (See Revised Statutes, Cap. 180, sections 126, 127 and 138; and Cap. 23, section 18.)

There are now 123 townships open for location as Free Grants, and these are divided into 16 agencies. The following is a list of the townships, with the names and addresses of the local agents, and directions how to reach the said agencies :—

1. MUSKOKA AGENCY.

This agency contains nineteen townships, viz.:

Baxter,	Monck,	Sinclair,
Brunel,	Morrison,	Stephenson,
Chaffey,	Muskoka,	Stisted,
Draper,	McLean,	Watt,
Franklin,	Oakley,	Wood.
Macaulay,	Ridout,	
Medora,	Ryde,	

Agent—Theo. C. Taylor, Bracebridge.

The route, in summer, is from Toronto to Gravenhurst by the Northern Railway, and from Gravenhurst to Bracebridge and the ports on Lakes Muskoka, Rosseau and Joseph, by steamer. In winter, the route from Gravenhurst is by stage.

2. PARRY SOUND AGENCY

Contains fourteen townships, viz.:

Cardwell,	Hagerman,	Mackenzie,
Carling,	Humphry,	McKellar,
Christie,	Montcith,	Shawanaga,
Fergusson,	McConkey,	Wilson,
Foley,	McDougall,	

Agent—Mrs. Theresa Mackay, Parry Sound.

In summer, the best route is from Toronto to Collingwood by the Northern Railway and thence to Parry Sound by steamer. In winter, from Toronto to Gravenhurst by railway and thence to Parry Sound by stage.

3. MAGANETAWAN AGENCY.

Contains eleven townships, viz.:

Chapman,	Lount,	Ryerson,
Croft,	Machar,	Spence,
Ferrie,	Mills,	Strong.
Gurd,	Pringle,	

Agent—S. G. Best, Maganetawan, which is situated on the Rosseau and Nipissing Road, in Chapman Township.

The route is from Toronto to Gravenhurst by railway in summer, from there to Rosseau by steamer, and thence to Maganetawan by stage. In winter, from Gravenhurst to Maganetawan by stage.

4. EAST PARRY SOUND AGENCY.

Contains six townships, viz.:

Armour,	Joly,	Perry.
Bethune,	McMurrich,	Proudfoot.

Agent—E. Handy, Emsdale, which is situated in the Township of Perry.

The route is by railway and steamer to Bracebridge, and thence by stage to Huntsville and Emsdale.

5. NIPISSING AGENCY.

Contains four townships, viz.:

Hardy,	Nipissing,	Patterson.
Himsworth,		

Agent—J. S. Scarlett, Nipissing.

The route is by railway and steamer to Rósseau, and thence to Maganetawan and Nipissing by stage.

---

6. MINDEN AGENCY

Contains seven townships, viz.:

Anson,	Lutterworth,	Stanhope,
Glamorgan,	Minden,	Snowdon.
Hindon,		

Agent—William Fielding, Minden.

The route is from Toronto to Coboconk by the Midland Railway, and thence to Minden by stage ; or from Toronto or Port Hope to Kinmount, by the same railway, and thence to Minden by stage.

---

7. HALIBURTON AGENCY

Contains four Townships, viz.:

Galway,	McClure,	Wicklow.
Bangor.		

Agent—Charles R. Stewart, Haliburton.

The route is from Port Hope or Toronto to Haliburton by the Midland Railway.

---

8. PETERBOROUGH OR BURLEIGH ROAD AGENCY.

Contains four townships, viz. :

Anstruther,	Cardiff,	Monmouth.
Chandos,		

Agent—D. Anderson, Apsley, in the Township of Anstruther.

The route is from Toronto or Port Hope to Lakefield by the Midland Railway, thence to Apsley by stage.

9. NORTH HASTINGS AGENCY

Contains nine townships, viz. :

Carlow,	Faraday,	Mayo,
Cashel,	Herschel,	Monteagle,
Dungannon,	Limerick,	Wollaston,

Agent—J. R. Tait, L'Amable, in the Township of Dungannon.

The route is from Belleville by the Belleville and North Hastings Railway, and by stage.

10. FRONTENAC AND ADDINGTON AGENCY

Contains seven townships, viz. :—

Abinger,	Clarendon,	Miller,
Canoto, South,	Denbigh,	Palmerston.
" North,		

Agent—G. W. Dawson, Plevna, in the Township of Clarendon.

The route is from Kingston, by the Kingston and Pembroke Railway, and by stage.

11. NORTH RENFREW AGENCY

Contains ten townships, viz. —

Alice,	Maria,	Wylie,
Buchanan,	McKay,	Pembroke and Mattawan
Fraser,	Petewawa,	Road.
Head,	Rolph,	

Agent—A. Kennedy, Pembroke.

The route is from Ottawa or Brockville to Pembroke by the Canadian Pacific Railway.

12. CENTRE RENFREW AGENCY

Contains seven townships, viz. :—

North Algona,	Hagarty,	Sherwood,
South "	Richards,	Wilberforce.
Grattan,		

Agent—James Reeves, Eganville.

The route is from Brockville to Cobden by the Canadian Pacific Railway, and thence to Eganville by stage.

13. SOUTH RENFREW AGENCY

Contains eight townships, viz. :—

Brougham,	Lyndock,	Raglan,
Brudenell,	Matawatchan,	Sebastopol.
Griffith,	Radcliffe,	

Agent—John Mahon, Vanbrugh, in the Township of Sebastopol.

The route is from Brockville or Ottawa to Cobden by the Canadian Pacific Railway, and thence to Vanbrugh by stage.

14. BRUCE MINES AGENCY

Contains two townships, viz. :—

Plummer,   St. Joseph's Island.*

Agent—John F. Day, Bruce Mines.

The route is from Toronto to Collingwood by the Northern Railway, and thence by steamer to the Bruce Mines.

15. SAULT STE. MARIE AGENCY

Contains four townships, viz. :—

| Aweres, | Parke, | Prince. |
| Korah, | | |

Agent—Charles P. Brown, Sault Ste. Marie.

The route is from Toronto to Collingwood by railway, and thence to the Sault by steamer.

16. THUNDER BAY AGENCY

Contains five townships, viz. :—

| Blake, | Dawson Road, | Paipoonge. |
| Crooks, | Oliver, | |

Agent—Amos Wright, Port Arthur.

The route is from Toronto to Collingwood by railway, and thence by steamer to Thunder Bay.

It will be observed that nearly all of these townships—112 out of the 123, which are now open under the Free Grants Act—are situated within

---

* Alexander G. Duncan, Marksville, is now Agent for St. Joseph Island.

what is known as the Huron and Ottawa Territory, or that territory lying between the Ottawa River and the Georgian Bay. This territory contains about 9,000,000 acres of land, and about 7,500,000 acres of it are surveyed. The 112 townships within it, which are open for location, contain about 4,883,000 acres, and about 2,100,000 acres have been already disposed of, leaving about 2,783,000 acres still unlocated.

As new townships are required for settlement, they will no doubt be placed in the market.

In case a party should desire to purchase public land which has been surveyed, but is not within the jurisdiction of any Crown Land agent, he should make his application direct to the Department, and support it by the affidavits of at least two credible and disinterested persons. These affidavits should set out all facts in connection with the land which he seeks to purchase, and especially whether it has ever been occupied, whether occupied at the time the application is made, and, if so, by whom, and when such occupation commenced; whether any improvements have been made on said land, and, if so, the nature and extent of the same, and by whom and when they were made; and also, whether there is any claim made thereto adverse to that of the applicant, and based on the ground of occupation or improvements. If the applicant has acquired the interest or claim of some previous occupant, he should show the fact and file an assignment.

MINERAL LANDS.

Public lands, which are open for sale, may be sold under "The General Mining Act" (Revised Statutes of Ontario, Cap. 29), at the rate of one dollar per acre cash. The patent is issued upon payment, and contains a reservation of all pine trees standing or being on the land. The pine continues to be the property of the Crown, who may at any time issue a license to cut it, and the party holding the license is empowered to enter at all times upon the land, cut and remove it, and make all necessary roads for that purpose.

Applications to purchase land under the Mining Act should be made direct to the Department, and should be accompanied by the purchase money, together with affidavits of at least two credible and disinterested parties, showing that the land is unoccupied and unimproved (except by or on behalf of the applicant), and that there is no claim thereto adverse to his on the ground of occupation, improvements or otherwise.

SYSTEM OF SURVEY.

The following diagram shows the form of a township as laid out in the Huron and Ottawa territory, or that territory between the Ottawa River

DIAGRAM.

and the Georgian Bay. It is divided into lots and concessions, but the lots are sometimes numbered from the East side of the township instead of from the West as shown in the figure.

The Surveyor is instructed to trace all the lines in the middle of the road allowances, and to plant posts at the distance of fifty links from the lines on both sides thereof. From the posts that he plants, he is to take the course and distance to the nearest tree, which he is to blaze in a conspicuous manner and mark " B. T." (Boundary Tree), and to enter the courses and distances of these trees from the posts in his field-book. Where a tree stands in the place for a post, he is to blaze it on four sides and mark it as he would the post. Where they can be had, he is to place stones round the posts at the corners of the township.

The regular farm lots are twenty chains in breadth by fifty chains in depth, and contain one hundred acres each. There is an allowance for road of one chain in width between each alternate concession and every fifth and sixth lot.

GENERAL DIRECTIONS.

Parties having business to transact with the Department of Crown Lands will save time and trouble by paying a little attention to the follow ind directions :

1. All communications on official business should be addressed to the Head of the Department, as follows :

THE HONOURABLE

THE COMMISSIONER OF CROWN LANDS,

TORONTO.

and the postage must be prepaid.

2. Letters on official business should not be addressed to the head or any officer of the Department by name, as such letters are considered private, and in the absense of the person so addressed will remain unopened.

3. Each letter should be confined to one subject, the post-office address should be given, and the signature distinctly written. In every subsequent letter the number of the lot and concession, and the name of the township should be repeated.

4. Where application is made for letters patent, the applicant should give his name in full, with place of residence and occupation, so that they may be set out in the patent ; and in case the applicant be a married woman, the name, residence and occupation of her husband should also be given.

5. In case a patent has been lost or destroyed, the party interested in the land may obtain either an exemplification or a certified copy of such patent by making application to the Hon. The Provincial Registrar. The fees for same are $8.25 for the former, and $2.50 for the latter, which should accompany the application.

6. Affidavits required in land matters may be made before any Crown Land Agent, Commissioner for taking affidavits, or Justice of the Peace.

7. When wills or assignments are sent to the Department, their execution must be attested by the affidavit of the subscribing witness.

8. When application is made to the Department for a fractional part of a lot for any purpose, such as a site for a school, church, cemetery, etc., the applicant should furnish a plan of the same by a Provincial Land Surveyor, showing its connection with the original survey, giving bearings and distances of the sides, and if broken by lake or river, the traverse lines by which the area was determined ; and also a description, by metes and bounds, of said fractional part by the Surveyor, for insertion in the patent. If the title to the lot of which it is a part be still in the Crown, the applicant must show by affidavit that there is no adverse claim on the ground of occupation or improvements, and if it be sold or located, an assignment from the owner must be filed.

9. In remitting money to the Department, it may be deposited in any branch of the Canadian Bank of Commerce, the Ontario Bank, the Quebec Bank, or the Bank of Montreal, and the draft and certificate sent by Mail to the Commissioner of Crown Lands, Toronto ; or if there be no agency of any of these banks convenient, it may be sent by post office order. Money remitted by letter is at the risk of the sender.

THE attention of all whom it may conce n is called to the following recited Act of the Legislature of Ontario, and they are hereby enjoined strictly to comply with its requirements, and observe the restrictions therein set forth with respect to setting out or starting fires during the period prescribed in said Act within the limits of any territory set apart as, and declared by proclamation in the *Ontario Gazette* to be a "Fire District;" and it is hereby notified that any person or persons neglecting or refusing to comply with the provisions of the Statute, or in any way contravening the same will be rigidly prosecuted, and on conviction punished with the utmost rigour of the law.

T. B. PARDEE,
Commissioner of Crown Lands.

DEPARTMENT OF CROWN LANDS,
    TORONTO, 27th March, 1878.

STATUTES OF ONTARIO, 41 VIC., CAP. 23.

An Act to preserve the Forests from destruction by Fire.

[*Assented to 7th March*, 1878.]

WHEREAS large quantities of valuable timber are an- Preamble. nually destroyed by fires which are in many instances the result of negligence and carelessness, it is therefore necessary to provide stringent regulations for the prevention of such fires.

Therefore Her Majesty, by and with the advice and consent of the Legislative Assembly of the Province of Ontario, enacts as follows :—

1. The Lieutenant-Governor, may, by proclamation to be Lt.-Governor made by him from time to time, issued by and with the advice may proclaim and consent of the Executive Council, declare any portion or a fire district. part of the Province of Ontario to be a fire district.

Publication of fire district.

2. Every proclamation under this Act shall be published in the *Ontario Gazette*, and such portion or part of the Province as is mentioned and declared to be a fire district in and by the said proclamation, shall, from and after the said publication, become a fire district within the meaning and for the purposes of this Act.

Revocation.

3. Every such portion or part of the Province mentioned in such proclamation, shall cease to be a fire district upon the revocation by the Lieutenant-Governor in Council of the proclamation by which it was created.

Fires not to be started except for certain purposes and in certain periods.

4. It shall not be lawful for any person to set out, or cause to be set out or started, any fire in or near the woods within any fire district, between the first day of April and the first day of November in any year, except for the purpose of clearing land, cooking, obtaining warmth, or for some industrial purpose ; and in cases of starting fires for any of the above purposes, the obligations and precautions imposed by the following sections shall be observed.

Precautions to be taken in case of clearing land.

5. Every person who shall between the first day of April and the first day of November, make or start a fire within such fire district for the purpose of clearing land, shall exercise and observe every reasonable care and precaution in the making and starting of such fire, and in the managing of and caring for the same after it has been made and started, in order to prevent such fire from spreading and burning up the timber and forests surrounding the place where it has been so made and started.

Precautions in case of cooking, &c.

6. Every person who shall between the first day of April and the first day of November, make or start within such fire district a fire in the forest, or at a distance of less than half-a-mile therefrom, or upon any Island for cooking, obtaining warmth, or for any industrial purpose, shall—

1. Select a locality in the neighbourhood in which there is the smallest quantity of vegetable matter, dead wood, branches, brushwood, dry leaves, or resinous trees ;

2. Clear the place in which he is about to light the fire by removing all vegetable matter, dead trees, branches, brushwood, and dry leaves from the soil within a radius of ten feet from the fire ;

3. Exercise and observe every reasonable care and precaution to prevent such fire from spreading, and carefully extinguish the same before quitting the place.

7. Any person who shall throw or drop any burning match, ashes of a pipe, lighted cigar or any other burning substance, or who shall discharge any firearm within such fire district shall be subject to the pains and penalties imposed by this Act, if he neglect completely to extinguish before leaving the spot the fire of such match, ashes of a pipe, cigar, wadding of the firearm or other burning substance.

Precautions in cases of matches, burning substances, etc.

8. Every person in charge of any drive of timber, survey or exploring party, or of any other party requiring camp-fires for cooking or other purposes within such fire district, shall provide himself with a copy of this Act, and shall call his men together and cause said Act to be read in their hearing, and explained to them at least once in each week during the continuance of such work or service.

Act to be read to employees by heads of surveys, lumberers, etc.

9. All locomotive engines used on any railway which passes through any such fire district or any part of it, shall, by the company using the same, be provided with and have in use all the most approved and efficient means used to prevent the escape of fire from the furnace or ash-pan of such engines, and that the smoke-stack of each locomotive engine so used shall be provided with a bonnet or screen of iron or steel wire-netting, the size of the wire used in making the netting to be not less than number nineteen of the Birmingham wire guage, or three sixty-fourth parts of an inch in diameter, and shall contain in each inch square at least eleven wires each way at right angles to each other, that is in all twenty-two wires to the inch square.

Precautions as to locomotives.

10. It shall be the duty of every engine driver in charge of a locomotive engine passing over any such railway within the limits of any such fire district, to see that all such appliances as are above-mentioned are properly used and applied, so as to prevent the unnecessary escape of fire from any such engine as far as it is reasonably possible to do so.

Duty of engine drivers.

11. Whosoever unlawfully neglects or refuses to comply with the requirements of this Act in any manner whatsoever, shall be liable upon a conviction before any justice of the peace to a penalty not exceeding fifty dollars, over and above the costs of prosecution, and in default of payment of such fine and costs, the offender shall be imprisoned in the common gaol for a period not exceeding three calendar months ; and any railway company permitting any locomotive engine to be run in violation of the provisions of the ninth section of this Act shall be liable to a penalty of one hundred dollars for each offence, to be recovered with costs in any court of competent jurisdiction.

Penalty for non-compliance with this Act.

5

Time for bringing action.

12. Every suit for any contravention of this Act shall be commenced within three calendar months immediately following such contravention.

Disposal of fines.

13. All fines and penalties imposed and collected under this Act shall be paid one-half to the complainant or prosecutor and the other half to Her Majesty for the public use of the Province.

Government agents to enforce this Act.

14. It shall be the special duty of every Crown Land agent, Woods and Forest agent, Free Grant agent, and bush ranger, to enforce the provisions and requirements of this Act, and in all cases coming within the knowledge of any such agent or bush ranger to prosecute every person guilty of a breach of any of the provisions and requirements of the same.

Act not to interfere with right of action for damages occasioned by fire.

15. Nothing in this Act contained shall be held to limit or interfere with the right of any party to bring and maintain a civil action for damages occasioned by fire, and such right shall remain and exist as though this Act had not been passed.